# NEW YORK'S
# UNIQUE
## & UNEXPECTED
# PLACES

# NEW YORK'S UNIQUE & UNEXPECTED PLACES

BY JUDITH STONEHILL
& ALEXANDRA STONEHILL

FOREWORD BY ETHAN HAWKE

UNIVERSE

FOR JOHN

# FOREWORD

## BY ETHAN HAWKE

"It's a myth, the city, the rooms and windows, the
steam spitting streets; for anyone, everyone,
a different myth, an idol-head with traffic light
eyes winking a tender green, a cynical red.
This island, floating in river water like a diamond
iceberg, call it New York, name it whatever you like;
the name hardly matters because entering
from the greater reality of elsewhere, one is only
in search of a city, a place to hide, to lose
or discover oneself, to make a dream wherein you
prove that perhaps after all you are not an
ugly duckling, but wonderful and worthy of love."

Truman Capote

At eighteen years of age, I dropped out of college and moved to New York City. It was 1989. The city was scary to me at that moment. The lower East Side seemed to have drugs sweating from its pores. Prostitutes actually walked the streets. You could see them in their fur coats and garter belts purring around the fountain in front of the Plaza Hotel—and that was the "nice" part of town. Brooklyn was as far away as Istanbul. Walking up from the subway at Times Square was like stumbling into a gang fight. That's what it *felt* like to me. What is strange is that I LOVED it. I loved it all. It was humanity on full display: pimples, sweat, love, heartbreak, addiction, brilliance, despair, and bliss. It was terrifying, but it was genuine and without pretense. There was no doubt that when you stood with both feet in NYC you were in the center of the universe.

The authenticity is harder to see these days, as the world seems to be owned entirely by three or four people. The same chain restaurants, newspapers, TV shows, video games and advertisements follow us everywhere. We are never lost. The computer in our pocket vibrates and there is somewhere we are "supposed" to be. We are made to be comfortable at all moments but, for me, there still is that scratchy feeling in my gut where I long to see under the surface, to know, and to be known. If I'm not lost how can I be found? Without fear how will I be courageous? I want to stay up late, high from the connection I've made with another traveler on the road. To see deep into someone's eyes, not just hung up on the eye "make up" or the "face-lift," but to see something real.

It's all still here—it's just hiding—like we are.

# INTRODUCTION

BY JUDITH STONEHILL

*New York's Unique & Unexpected Places* is written for urban ramblers who want to explore fascinating but less familiar sites in the city. Discover — and sometimes rediscover — secluded gardens, idiosyncratic museums, little shops here and there, and the occasional well-known place with distinctive treasures.

Enjoy the dazzling contrasts within the city: the unfolding perspectives seen from a park in the sky or from the front porch of an eighteenth-century farmhouse. Visit a wildlife refuge, an innovative center for architecture, and an extraordinary map collection. Roam through small museums dedicated to skyscrapers, finance, sculpture, and fashion. Listen to the urban cacophony of melodious songbirds, poetry read aloud, the sounds of jazz, and the chatter of some 170 languages spoken by the city's inhabitants.

Observe the river traffic from a waterfront boardwalk or from the lawn of a Victorian cottage. Notice the details that give each area a sense of place: the diverse shops, a surprising number of little parks, and the sidewalk choreography that varies from one neighborhood to the next. Spend time at places of inspiration: a sculptor's studio, a tranquil chapel, a garden of stones. Note the clouds tangled between buildings during the day and the soaring towers illuminated each night.

This guidebook aims to coax readers to venture beyond New York's major attractions and become acquainted with some of the city's more uncommon corners. The fifty destinations included here could easily have been hundreds, and it's hoped that readers will create their own lists of favorites (and describe these in the blank page at the end of the book). More than forty-seven million visitors come to New York each year, mingling with the city's eight million residents, yet the possibilities of finding unique and unexpected places are endless in this incomparable, astonishing city.

# LOWER
# MANHATTAN

# IRISH HUNGER MEMORIAL

North End Avenue at Vesey Street
Battery Park City

www.batteryparkcity.org

HOURS: Daily 8:30 am to dusk
(except in severe weather)

Stones from each of Ireland's thirty-two
counties are scattered across the landscape.

**D**esigned with a dual purpose, the Irish Hunger Memorial commemorates the tragedy of the Irish famine of 1845–52 while also reminding us of the very real problem of global hunger today. Part of the site is planted with clover in fallow potato ridges. These symbolize the empty harvests that plagued the country after blight destroyed the potato crops, creating the catastrophic famine that caused the deaths of hundreds of thousands and forced the migration of tens of thousands more.

Winding paths lead through a half-acre green landscape, past stone walls and an abandoned cottage surrounded by Irish plants. How surprised this small house must be, to find itself so far away from County Mayo. Taken apart, stone

by stone, the roofless dwelling—originally built in the 1820s—was brought across the Atlantic and reconstructed here.

The landscape changes with the seasons. Burnet roses are planted here, along with gorse, heather, blackthorn, heath, wild yellow iris, and foxglove—all originating from the Connact boglands. Everything has an Irish origin, including the large stones scattered about, each from one of Ireland's thirty-two counties. The hillside is cantilevered over a base of glass and green-grey Kilkenny limestone strewn with fossils from an ancient Irish seabed. Walking up the path, visitors feel as though they're in the countryside until they arrive at the top of the hill, where an overlook offers sweeping views of New York harbor.

The memorial's designer, the sculptor Brian Tolle, describes the site as "a little fragment of Ireland built on a heap of language." Layers of text wrap around the exterior of the memorial and into the passageway leading to the cottage. The words are taken from letters and memoirs, parliamentary reports, parish records, recipes, newspaper accounts, songs, and statistics, all poignantly linking the nineteenth-century Irish famine to the continued problem of world hunger.

*Above and opposite: An evocative perspective of Irish plants and stones.*

# POETS HOUSE

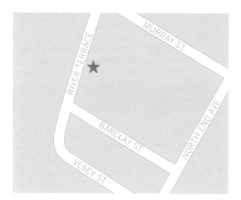

Ten River Terrace
(between Murray and Vesey Streets)
Battery Park City

212.431.7920
www.poetshouse.org

HOURS: Tuesday–Friday 11 am–7 pm;
Saturday 11 am–6 pm
(hours may be extended, so check website)

*I reckon—when I count at all*
*First—Poets—Then the Sun—*
*Then Summer—Then the Heaven*
*of God—*
*And then—the List is done—*

*But looking back—the First so seems*
*To Comprehend the Whole*
*The Others look a needless Show—*
*So I write—Poets—All—*

Emily Dickinson

When Poets House began in 1985, the poet Stanley Kunitz—who was one of the founders—purposely chose to leave off the apostrophe on *poets* because "some things must never be possessed but shared." This inclusive, welcoming place is indeed open to everyone, inviting visitors to browse through its collection of books, listen to a poetry reading, or consider writing a poem, prompted by the oblique light slanting off the river.

Anyone who loves poetry or the mesmerizing power of words will be captivated by Poets House. Imagine a literary center with two floors of sun-filled spaces and a reading room overlooking the Hudson River, a library of more than 50,000 volumes, a priceless archive of poets' recordings and videos, a program hall for readings, an exhibition space

Opposite: Portraits of Walt Whitman and Marianne Moore juxtaposed to books by fellow poets.

cantilevered over the first floor, and a large whimsical children's room to inspire the next generation of poets.

Every April, in celebration of National Poetry Month, Poets House exhibits American poetry published during the past year. More than 2,000 titles are displayed—with the majority from independent presses—ranging from small 24-page chapbooks to lengthy anthologies. A whirlwind of activity takes place here throughout the year, with poetry festivals, master classes taught by outstanding poets, and a midsummer-night reading on the lawn outside. On Poem-in-Your-Pocket Day, hundreds of passengers receive a poem as they disembark at the nearby ferry terminal.

How appropriate that New York, the subject of so many poems, should possess a Poets House. Robert Lowell's poem "Central Park" and John Hollander's "West End Blues" pin the city to a certain place and time, as do Derek Walcott's "Spring Street in '58" and Amy Clampitt's "Times Square Water Music." Sometimes the titles sound like directions to a local taxi driver: "164 East 72nd Street" by James Merrill or "227 Waverly

Place" by W. S. Merwin or "209 Canal" by Richard Howard. The city's various transitions and moods, ready to change like quicksilver, are expressed in blank verse, sonnets, epics, odes, and perhaps an occasional villanelle. The poet Howard Moss perfectly described New York poems as "histories of desperation or hope; note-takings of the phenomenal; musings on loneliness, connection, isolation, joy."

Above: Photographic collage showing riverfront view from Poets House. Opposite: Volume of poetry and portrait of Edna St. Vincent Millay.

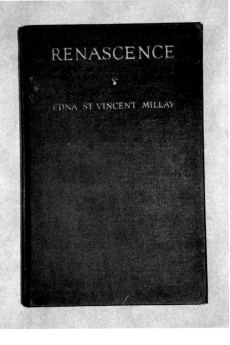

# THE SKYSCRAPER MUSEUM

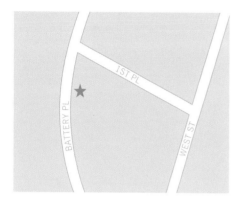

39 Battery Place
Entrance on the west side of
the Ritz-Carlton Hotel
Lower Manhattan

212.968.1961
www.skyscraper.org

HOURS: Wednesday–Sunday 12 pm–6 pm

Located near down-town's high-rise canyons, this small, marvelous museum inspires visitors to learn more about New York's architectural heritage.

It's an ideal starting point for exploring lower Manhattan: The area's long history is visible in the winding streets created by seventeenth-century Dutch settlers; centuries later, its skyline is filled with soaring towers.

The design of the Skyscraper Museum is ingenious: Although the space is limited to 5,000 square feet, there's much going on within this brilliantly devised interior. By using a reflective steel floor and ceiling panels to give the illusion of infinite height, the museum evokes the spirit and scale of a tall building "rising

Left: Endless reflections express the verticality of the museum gallery space. Opposite: Skyscraper Museum entrance ramp.

Upper left:
Photographs of the
Flatiron Building
under construction
and completed,
1901–1903.
Lower left: Riveting
steel on 86th floor
of the Empire
State Building,
August, 1930.

in sheer exaltation from bottom to top"—as architect Louis Sullivan poetically described high-rises.

Architects, engineers, contractors, building enthusiasts, urban historians, every schoolchild, and anyone eager to learn about the city will be fascinated by this collection of architectural drawings and blueprints, construction photographs, structural models, maps, films, and even a chunk of an 1890s I-beam. The museum is committed to interpreting the evolving history of the skyscraper and its future around the world. Recent exhibitions have juxtaposed an early twentieth-century American skyscraper city with twenty-first-century Chinese cities, comparing their parallel conditions of rapid urbanization.

The museum has even put skyscrapers in cyberspace. Its innovative Website presents a 3-D computer model of Manhattan so that anyone can zoom in on a neighborhood and explore particular buildings. Check out the Empire State Building, view its construction photographs from 1931, and learn that this enormous building—102 stories tall, with more than two million square feet—was built in just 410 days.

For those who are curious about how these high-rise structures came to be called skyscrapers, it seems that they were named after the clipper ships' main mast, or topmast, which was known in nautical terminology as a skyscraper. In those days, the height of ships' masts rivaled that of the spire of Trinity Church, until downtown's tall buildings soared ever higher. In the 1890s, a visiting British writer described the perpendicular life of the city: "When they find themselves a little crowded, they simply tilt the street on end and call it a skyscraper."

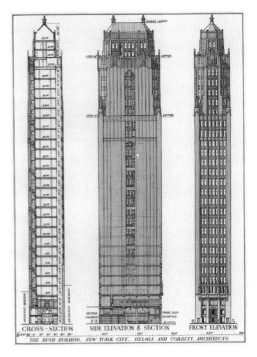

Above: Architectural drawings of Bush Tower on West 42nd Street, completed in 1918.

# GARDEN
# OF STONES

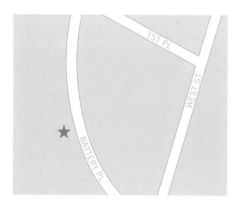

Museum of Jewish Heritage
36 Battery Place
Lower Manhattan

646.437.4200
www.mjhnyc.org

HOURS: Sunday–Tuesday, Thursday
10 am–5:45 pm; Wednesday 10 am–8 pm;
Friday 10 am–3 pm. Closed Saturdays,
Jewish holidays, Thanksgiving Day

Eighteen enormous boulders are placed so closely together that it's as if they've been dropped from the heavens into the extraordinary Garden of Stones. Varying in size from three tons to thirteen tons, the boulders have each been hollowed out, filled with earth, and planted with tiny oak saplings—Quercus prinoides—expected to grow into trees twelve feet tall within a few decades.

This contemplative space is dedicated to the memory of those who perished in the Holocaust and to honor those who survived. Located on the second-floor roof terrace of the Museum of Jewish Heritage, the garden was created by the sculptor Andy Goldsworthy, who brought together the immutable tawny grey boulders and the fragile saplings to represent the intertwining of life cycles.

Left and opposite: Each stone is said to be "ingrained with geological and historical memories."

The garden intricately connects memory and timelessness, hardship and tenacity, tragedy and hope. The sculptures recall the Jewish tradition of placing stones on a gravesite, letting the deceased know that someone was there to visit. That there are eighteen boulders is also symbolic. In Hebrew, every letter possesses a number; *chai*, whose number value is eighteen, is the Hebrew word for "life." There is meaning even in the disparate size of the boulders, as Goldsworthy has noted: "There is energy within a group of stones of various sizes. It becomes a family."

The Garden of Stones is meant to be revisited and experienced in different ways over time. The trees will grow, the stones will be warmed by sunlight and chilled by winter's snows; both trees and stones will adapt to foggy mornings and starlit nights. Those who visit the garden will find that its powerful imagery evokes a sense of wonder and gives new meaning to familiar objects. What is more elemental, after all, than trees and stones?

Below: The tiny oak saplings planted in boulders represent the intertwining of life cycles.

# MUSEUM OF AMERICAN FINANCE

48 Wall Street
(corner of William Street)
Lower Manhattan

212.908.4110
www.financialhistory.org

HOURS: Tuesday–Saturday 10 am–4 pm

Above: A nineteenth-century bond.

**W**all Street is the center of New York's financial district and known throughout the world as a symbol of capitalism and power. It's a perfect site for the Museum of American Finance, located a block away from the New York Stock Exchange. The museum is just down the street from the site of the first exchange, which was established under a buttonwood tree in 1792.

The museum exhibitions are geared to anyone interested in money: investors, historians, schoolchildren, MBAs, and the merely curious wondering how New York City evolved into a global powerhouse. There's much to see and learn here, with more than 10,000 items in the collection: federal currency issued by President Abraham Lincoln in 1861 to finance the Civil War; interactive interviews with twenty-first-century entrepreneurs;

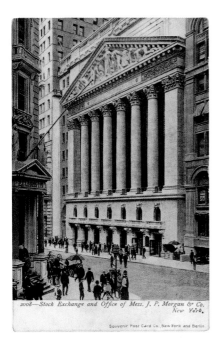

2008—Stock Exchange and Office of Mess. J. P. Morgan & Co.
New York.

Souvenir Post Card Co. New York and Berlin

a 60-pound ingot from the California Gold Rush; beautifully engraved stock certificates and rare currency, including a $10,000 bill; antique board games that allowed players to invest on Wall Street without risking losses; newspapers from October 1929 with headlines shouting: BILLIONS LOST IN WALL STREET DEBACLE.

The museum's 1929 building served as the home of the Bank of New York. This was the city's first bank, founded by Alexander Hamilton in 1784, a few months after the British troops ended their occupation of the city. A room in the museum is devoted to Hamilton, who created America's

financial system when he was the nation's first Secretary of the Treasury. Hamilton is undoubtedly one of the most recognizable of the Founding Fathers, with his portrait appearing on the $10 bill.

Whether the stock market is up or down when you visit, the museum is a fascinating place to get a wide-ranging perspective on the financial system and its cyclical nature. The vagaries of fortune are explored here: wild exuberance followed by market crashes, bulls metamorphosing into bears. When exploring the museum, keep in mind the words of Benjamin Franklin: "Who is rich? He that is content."

Right: The business magazine *Fortune*, founded in 1930, cost the high price of a dollar an issue at a time when the Sunday *New York Times* was only five cents.

Previous pages: Left: Interior of the Museum of American Finance. Right top: Vintage postcard of New York Stock Exchange. Right below: Detail of downtown skyscrapers.

Fortune
One Dollar a Copy    FEBRUARY 1933    Ten Dollars a Year

F.V. CARPENTER

# ELEVATED ACRE

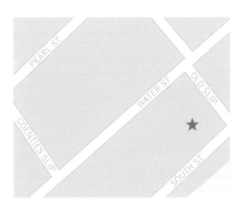

55 Water Street
(Between Old Slip and Coenties Slip)
Lower Manhattan

212.747.9120
www.elevatedacre.com

HOURS: May 1–September 30 7 am–10 pm;
October 1–April 30 8 am–8 pm

Above: The lawn of the Elevated Acre, with
the Police Museum in the background.

One of the most unexpected parks in the city is the Elevated Acre, located more than thirty feet above the East River waterfront.

Take the escalator or stairs to the plaza level at 55 Water Street, and there you'll encounter an engaging urban landscape in the sky.

Imagine finding twenty-five locust trees, dune grasses, and a profusion of wildflowers and plants in this small park. Woodland shrubs—viburnum, Ilex, oak-leaf hydrangea, and Amelanchier— are planted on the landward side, which offers less exposure to the gusty winds. Placed in shady corners are benches for reading or a picnic lunch; just beyond, a seven-tiered amphitheater surrounds a spacious lawn used for dance performances and outdoor movies on summer evenings.

Parallel to the East River, a sturdy boardwalk offers a panoramic view of the Brooklyn Bridge and the river traffic. At the north end

of the boardwalk, a 50-foot-tall light sculpture—a translucent glass lantern visible from afar—seems inspired by the navigation lights guiding the ships on the river.

The firms of Rogers Marvel Architects and Ken Smith Landscape Architecture created this space for a design competition held to revive the plaza. The challenge was daunting; enormous

buildings loom over the Elevated Acre, yet the configuration of the trees and plants gives the place a sense of scale and muffles the noise from the helicopters taking off and landing on the adjacent pier.

The park is privately owned but open to the public. The street one block to the north—Old Slip, where sailing ships once docked—is home to the Police Museum, located in what had been the First Precinct Police Station. Built in 1909, this impressive limestone structure and its red-tiled roof provide an interesting counterpoint to the green lawn of the Elevated Acre.

This quiet park is a refuge from the hectic offices and crowded streets of the financial district. Remember Herman Melville's *Bartleby the Scrivener?* Think of poor Bartleby, toiling a few blocks away on Wall Street, copying law papers by sunlight and candlelight, with only a view of a bleak brick wall. Perhaps he would have been less "prone to a pallid hopelessness" had he been able to spend some time at the Elevated Acre.

# BOWNE & COMPANY STATIONERS

South Street Seaport Museum
211 Water Street (between Fulton
and Beekman Streets)
Lower Manhattan

212.748.8651
www.southstreetseaportmuseum.org

HOURS: Tuesday–Sunday 10 am–5 pm

**B**owne & Company resembles a typical nineteenth-century print shop, with vintage treadle-powered presses—the earliest dating back to 1844—still used today for printing stationery, bookplates, valentines, business cards, and limited-edition volumes of Emily Dickinson's works. All of these are sold in the front of the shop, an *omnium-gatherum* of wonderful paper goods perched on the counter and shelves and even on the wooden cabinets filled with type.

The shop occupies the ground floor of a handsome brick Greek-revival building, whose large windows overlook pear trees and a street paved with Belgian blocks. Inside, the collection of working presses and trays of wood and metal type—with more than 1,200 typeface styles—are artfully organized by the master printer and curator, Robert Warner.

Left: Penmanship series printed by letterpress at Bowne & Company. Opposite: Storefront façade.

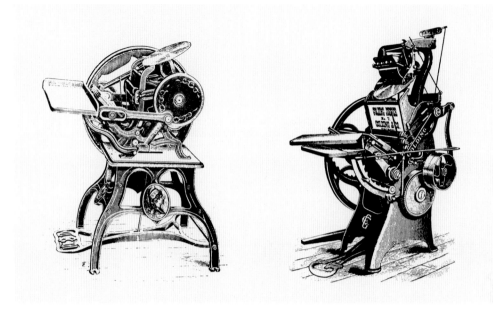

For those who are intrigued by the venerable platen presses and the joyful inventiveness of printing by hand, introductory classes in letterpress printing are taught here in the fall and spring.

Part of the South Street Seaport Museum, Bowne is just two blocks inland from the waterfront and the museum's collection of historic ships. It is a fitting location, near the nineteenth-century printing district, an area that once bustled with paper suppliers, type foundries, ink makers, bookbinders, and the many newspaper publishers located on nearby Park Row. Printers in those days were always busy creating bills of lading, advertising cards, and stock certificates for the local shipping and banking firms.

Bowne has been part of New York's history for more than two hundred years. In 1775, Robert Bowne opened a shop on Pearl Street, stocking its shelves with writing paper, accounting books, printing materials, and various dry goods. Eventually the company specialized in printing services for the financial district. Today, Bowne is the world's largest financial printer and a corporate sponsor of its descendent, Bowne & Company Stationers at the Seaport Museum.

Above left: 1878 Columbian Rotary Press.
Above right: 1901 Golding Jobber Press. Opposite: Typesetting tray and tools at Bowne & Company.

AMERICAN WOOD TYPE
MANUFACTURING COMPANY
STAR ★ TYPE
HORSFALL & SONS (STARTYPE) LTD.
BIRSTALL near BATLEY
WEST YORKSHIRE · ENGLAND
LOWER CASE

552
PRESS KNEE BACK
MADE BY
CHICAGO
U.S.A.

# LOWER EAST SIDE TO THE EAST VILLAGE

# ITALIAN AMERICAN MUSEUM

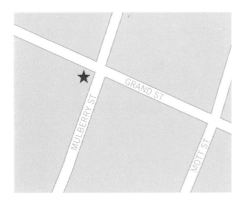

155 Mulberry Street
(corner of Grand and Mulberry Streets)
Little Italy/Chinatown

212.965.9000
www.italianamericanmuseum.org

HOURS: Wednesday–Sunday 11 am–6 pm;
Friday until 8 pm
(Hours may be extended, so call ahead)

Above: Exterior detail of the Italian
American Museum.

The Italian American Museum recently opened in the Banca Stabile building on Mulberry Street. Built in 1885, the structure still has the original tin ceilings, terrazzo floors, and tellers' windows dating from its days as a family-owned bank serving the Italian community. When restoring the building, museum officials discovered that the old vault contained unexpected treasures: bankbooks filled with handwritten transactions, vintage Italian *lire*, luggage tags from passenger ships, cablegrams, receipts, passports, and, mysteriously, a small revolver.

In those days, financial transactions were only part of what Banca Stabile offered. Translation services were provided for immigrants unable to read English, and even travel arrangements were available. (One of the tellers'

BANCA
MALZONE

windows is still inscribed with the words "Steamship Tickets" in gold lettering.) In the early years of immigration, many Italian men were called "birds of passage" because they traveled back and forth in pursuit of seasonal labor; it was worth making this arduous trip, since a steerage ticket between Naples and New York cost $15 in 1880.

A vast number of Italian immigrants from Sicily and southern Italy settled in New York from the 1880s through the first decade of the twentieth century. The newcomers tended to live near those from their own native village or region, mistrusting others as *forestieri*, or strangers. Block by block, the immigrants created enclaves of familiar customs and dialects. Mulberry Street belonged to the Neapolitans. Those from Calabria lived on Mott, the Pugliesi on Hester Street; immigrants from the western part of Sicily settled on Elizabeth and Prince Streets; and the eastern Sicilians lived on Catherine and Monroe Streets. It was said that "almost every block has its own village of mountain or lowland . . . and its patron saint."

Today there are fewer than a thousand Italians living in this neighborhood, but many others come back for nostalgic visits, accompanied by their children and grandchildren. The Italian American Museum provides yet another reason to return, offering a broad spectrum of exhibitions, lectures, art festivals, and educational programs related to the Italian immigrant experience. Plans are under way to re-create a Sicilian puppet theater, and a future initiative will trace the history of Italian opera in America. Still a work in progress, this small museum has large ambitions, as did the Italian immigrants who came to America and whose hopes and dreams are celebrated here.

Above: Receipts found in the original vault of Banca Stabile. Opposite: Detail from a handcolored photograph of Mulberry Street in 1900.

# MUSEUM OF CHINESE IN AMERICA

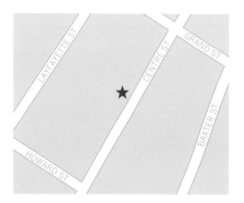

215 Centre Street
(Between Howard and Grand Streets)
Chinatown/Soho

212.619.4785
www.mocanyc.org

HOURS: Monday 11 am–5 pm;
Thursday 11 am–9 pm; Friday 11 am–5 pm;
Saturday and Sunday 10 am–5 pm

MOCA—as the Museum of Chinese in America is now called—recently moved to an impressive new space designed by Maya Lin. The bronze walls and enormous skylight illuminating a two-story interior courtyard present a bold contrast to the small crowded space that had been the museum's previous home, five blocks away. Chinatown long ago expanded its boundaries, and MOCA's new presence seems to be a perfect expression of the broadening Chinese cultural influence, both globally and in New York.

This is one of the most fascinating museums in the city. Visitors are attracted by its marvelously curated exhibitions,

its comprehensive collection of 60,000 items, its walking tours through Chinatown, and its film project featuring Chinatowns from all over the globe.

In presenting the history and culture of Chinese people in the United States, the museum tells a riveting story. During the late 1840s, the California gold rush drew the first group of Chinese to America. Many more came in the next decades to work in the mines in the frontier states or to help build the transcontinental railroad that would link the country from coast to coast. These early immigrants were known as "golden mountain uncles," or *gim sen lao*, by the families they'd left in China, who were supported by the backbreaking labor of those working here. Eventually, the Chinese workers scattered across

America, building railroads in Alabama and Louisiana, Texas and even Alaska, "banding the nation… with crisscrossing steel. They were the binding and building ancestors of this place."

Story by story, MOCA is gathering the testimony of Chinese Americans throughout the country as they recount their own experiences, those of their family, or even those of distant ancestors. The narratives are collected from letters and documents, oral histories, business records, newspapers, books, and manuscripts, along with family photographs and memorabilia. Each preserves a memory; together, they express the courage and determination, loneliness and rejection, heartbreak and triumph that have been part of the long journey from China to America.

Right above: Reversible robe for an immortal from the Chinese Musical and Theatrical Association Collection of MOCA. Right below: Architectural rendering of the MOCA entrance by Maya Lin Studio.

Previous page: Left: Chinese-English calendar. Right: Family portrait taken in 1927 in Portland, Oregon.

# MUSEUM AT ELDRIDGE STREET

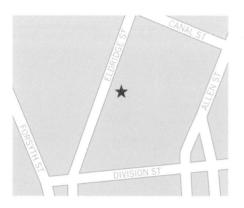

12 Eldridge Street
(Between Canal and Division Streets)
Lower East Side/Chinatown

212.219.0888
www.eldridgestreet.org

HOURS: Sunday–Thursday 10 am–4 pm

This beautiful build-ing, now known as the Museum at Eldridge Street, began life in 1887 as the first great synagogue built in America by eastern European Jews.

Its ornate facade combines Moorish, Gothic, and Romanesque elements, with striking Star of David patterns that proudly identify this structure as a Jewish house of worship.

At the time the synagogue was built, the Lower East Side teemed with a vast population of Jewish immigrants living in poverty and hardship. Yet even then it was a neighborhood of hopes and dreams and ambitious beginnings. Building this synagogue—as one architectural historian noted—was "a glorious testament to this

Left: Restoration of stained-glass windows in the Eldridge Street Museum. Opposite: The striking facade, with its Moorish, Gothic, and Romanesque details.

congregation's faith in the New World."

A century passed, the Jewish immigrants prospered and moved on, and the congregation dwindled until there were fewer than twenty members to support this enormous structure. By then, the building was plagued by a crumbling foundation, years of water damage from a leaky roof, and a desperate need to repair the once-exquisite sanctuary. "It was as though the synagogue was held up by strings from heaven," said Roberta Brandes Gratz, founder of the Eldridge Street Project, the organization responsible for the building's extraordinary restoration.

The main sanctuary, with its glorious seventy-foot-high vaulted ceiling, is once again elaborately adorned in Moorish designs: azure skies studded with gold-leaf stars, intertwining floral motifs, and trompe l'oeil murals of curtained windows overlooking Jerusalem. The sixty-seven stained-glass windows, made up of more than 250 panels, have also been restored. All of the original Victorian brass light fixtures and the central chandelier, composed of more than 400 parts, have been returned to their original splendor.

The Museum at Eldridge Street welcomes people of all backgrounds and offers many educational programs, tours, and exhibits focusing on the immigrant experience. This is still a neighborhood of newcomers, and the current population is mainly Chinese. However, Orthodox Jewish services are still held on Friday nights and Saturdays in the study hall downstairs, where the synagogue's original wooden ark is kept.

Take time also to visit the fascinating Lower East Side Tenement Museum, a few blocks away at 108 Orchard Street. Once crammed with immigrant families, the tenement's tiny rooms are a remarkable contrast to the impressive sanctuary on Eldridge Street. For many of the new settlers, worshipping in this sanctuary was not only a spiritual experience, but also a refuge and a haven—a sanctuary in the truest sense—from the tumultuous world outside.

_Opposite: The main sanctuary, with its spectacular seventy-foot-high vaulted ceiling._

# HUA MEI BIRD GARDEN

W ho would expect to find rare songbirds giving concerts in this unlikely corner of the city? Just south of Delancey Street, inside Sara Delano Roosevelt Park, the Hua Mei Bird Garden is the gathering place each morning for a group of Chinese men and their treasured birds.

Hua Mei birds are famous for their singing. Imported at great cost from Asia, each has its own particular songs; birds with a large repertoire are much more valuable than those producing only a few tunes. The singing sounds like a musical dialogue between the birds, with their warbling, trilling, and chirping

*A bird does not sing because it has an answer.*
*It sings because it has a song.*

Chinese proverb

rising to a crescendo as they skitter about their bamboo cages.

The garden is open only to the Hua Mei Bird Club, but passersby are welcome to sit on an adjacent stone wall with the Chinese men—the club members—whose numbers vary depending on the weather. This coming-together of songbirds and owners is an ancient tradition in China, although the ritual of competition seems good-natured in this bird garden. The owners discuss and compare the plumage of the birds, the elegance of each handmade cage, and, always, the power of the singing.

Hua Mei birds are small, with russet brown feathers. Their name, *hua mei*, translates literally as "painted eyebrows," referring to the distinctive white circle around their eyes. Legend has it that these birds were trained to sing during the Ming dynasty. Centuries later, in New York, their amazing singing can drown out the tumult and noise of Delancey Street's traffic and marvelously create a tranquil morning haven.

Sara Delano Roosevelt Park
Delancey Street
(between Chrystie and Forsyth Streets)
Lower East Side

HOURS: Mornings only, usually 7 am–12 pm

Above: Hua Mei birds during a morning concert.

# ECONOMY CANDY

108 Rivington Street
(Between Essex
and Ludlow Streets)
Lower East Side

800.352.4544
www.economycandy.com

OPEN HOURS: Sunday–Friday 9 am–6 pm;
Saturday 10 am–5 pm

This must be one of the last places on earth to find Jumbo Jaw Breakers. Or Pop Rocks. Economy Candy specializes in treats remembered from childhood. Sugar Babies, Pixy Stix, candy cigarettes, whirly pops, wax lips (Wack-O-Wax lips, to be exact), multicolored candy buttons, Charleston Chews, giant Twizzlers, Necco wafers, kosher jelly beans, Fleer's double-bubble gum, salted licorice, and Atomic Fireballs, to name just a few.

This old-fashioned store is jam-packed, floor to ceiling, with all these candies, along with dried fruits, a variety of nuts, hand-dipped chocolates, and more than a dozen kinds of halvah. Everything is discounted. Economy Candy has been a fixture on the Lower East Side since 1937, still family owned and still selling the kind of candy you don't find anywhere else.

You may or may not have a Proustian experience when taking a bite of their chocolate-covered graham crackers. Owner Jerry Cohen can't guarantee *that*, but he does claim: "If someone needs to be cheered up, they come here."

Above and opposite: Old-fashioned sweets.

# RUSS & DAUGHTERS

How do you define a legend? Russ & Daughters is described by food mavens as a "hallowed shrine to the miracle of caviar and smoked salmon." The display cases at this small family-owned shop are filled with a dozen different kinds of heavenly smoked salmon and rows of equally celestial herring, whitefish, black cod, smoked sturgeon, and chopped liver. The caviar selection is irresistible, as is the handmade Russian blini.

Near the entrance, barrels of pickles and baskets of bagels remind one of the Lower East Side in the old days. It was then a densely populated community of poor Jewish immigrants; now the area has been reinvented as a fashionable and expensive neighborhood. It's no wonder that the Smithsonian Institution has acclaimed Russ & Daughters for being part of the city's cultural heritage for nearly a century.

Like all legends, it's best to begin—as did Russ & Daughters—with a strong story line. An immigrant arrives in America from eastern Europe in 1900, acquires a pushcart to peddle herring on the city streets, and in 1914 opens a store on the Lower East Side. The immigrant—Joel Russ—then brings his three attractive daughters into the store, eventually makes them partners, and the business prospers. Another generation, and still another, decide to continue this tradition so that today the fourth generation of the Russ family—the young cousins Joshua Russ Tupper and Niki Russ Federman—run this fabled establishment.

The store is so beloved that one loyal customer requested a special order when he was ready to propose marriage to his girlfriend. A favorite sandwich— a bagel with whitefish and baked salmon salad, horseradish cream cheese, and wasabi flying fish roe—was suitably gift-wrapped; the ring was tied to the ribbon strung around the sandwich. And of course she said yes.

179 Houston Street
(Between Orchard and Allen Streets)
Lower East Side

212.475.4880
www.russanddaughters.com

HOURS: Monday–Friday 8 am–8 pm;
Saturday 9 am–7 pm; Sunday 8 am–5:30 pm

Above: Note the welcoming salmon on the pink
and green neon exterior sign. Step inside the
store for Russ & Daughters' caviar.

# PAGEANT PRINT SHOP

**B**eyond the bright blue door of this small shop are thousands of vintage prints and maps. Botanical prints, political cartoons, advertising bills, sheet music, and architectural drawings are organized into their own sections. Racks of hand-colored prints of seashells, sailing ships, and exotic birds are close at hand to nineteenth-century maps and views of New York and cities across the world.

Pageant Print Shop descended from the famous "Book Row" on Fourth Avenue, once the location of several dozen second-hand booksellers. In 1946, Sidney Solomon and Henry Chafetz—both veterans just back from World War II—opened Pageant Book Company at 59 Fourth Avenue. They specialized in books on art, literature, and Americana, along with a collection of vintage prints and maps.

It's still a family business, now owned by Solomon's daughters, Shirley and Rebecca. The emphasis these days is definitely on prints and maps, although they're happy to search for out-of-print books and pamphlets, too. Collectors—as well as those just looking for a unique birthday present—appreciate the affordable prices.

After moving a few times over the decades, Pageant is now happily ensconced in the East Fourth Street arts district, where it is surrounded by theaters and dance companies. Moviegoers still remember when, in 1986, Pageant—located several blocks north at the time—was featured in Woody Allen's film *Hannah and Her Sisters*. The shop was easily recognized by its bold blue facade back then, just as it is today.

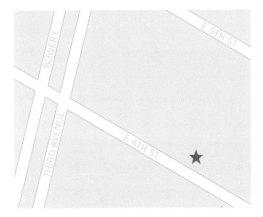

69 East 4th Street
(Between Second and Third Avenues)
East Village

212.674.5296
www.pageantprintshop.com

OPEN: Tuesday–Saturday 12 pm–8 pm;
Sunday 1 pm–7 pm

Top: Victorian engraving of a bird, part of
the Pageant Print Shop's collection. Bottom:
The blue storefront. Opposite: Map from late
nineteenth century.

# MERCHANT'S HOUSE MUSEUM

29 East 4th Street
(Between Lafayette and Bowery)
East Village

212.777.1089
www.merchantshouse.org

HOURS: Thursday–Monday 12 pm–5 pm

I magine a row of elegant nineteenth-century houses where now there is only one. This remarkable survivor—the Merchant's House Museum—vividly evokes a long-ago time in New York. Open its front gate, walk up the white marble steps, and enter the well-preserved home of the Tredwell family, who lived here for nearly a century.

Seabury Tredwell, a wealthy merchant, purchased the house in 1835, three years after it was built. At the time, this was a fashionable neighborhood of the *haute bourgeoisie*. The Tredwells and their eight children fit right into this world, with their Duncan Phyfe furniture and crimson silk curtains, bronze candelabra, and Staffordshire china.

Architectural styles were evolving from Federal to Greek revival at the time the house was built, so both styles are in evidence here. The exterior is typical of late Federal houses,

with its sedate red-brick facade, dark painted shutters, and delicate iron railing. The elegant doorway is richly detailed with narrow Ionic columns and an exquisite fanlight over the arched door, irresistibly drawing visitors inside. And beyond the door? A perfect Greek-revival interior, with formal double parlors, black marble mantelpieces, high ceilings decorated with lavish plasterwork, and matching gas chandeliers from the 1830s.

The fascination of this house, outside and in, is that it exists as a family history of the Tredwells. The house is preserved with the chairs they sat on and the piano they played, the beds they slept in and the books they read. The closets hold more than 400 items belonging to the Tredwell ladies: bonnets and laces, paisley shawls, hand-embroidered dresses, tiny satin shoes, and a wedding gown with a headdress of orange blossoms.

Walking through these rooms filled with the Tredwells' possessions makes you think of the family, but most of all you think of Gertrude. The youngest of the children, she was born in the house in 1840 and died in the same bedroom in 1933, having lived in the house her entire life. She outlived all of her family and even her surroundings;

by then the genteel neighborhood had become an area "hemmed in by ugliness and forgotten." Dear Gertrude, why didn't you keep a diary during all those years? Perhaps it doesn't matter, for the house, in every detail, tells her story.

Above: Detail of a Tredwell family possession. Opposite: View of the garden, as seen from the tea room on the parlor floor.

Previous page: Right: Detail of the Merchant's House parlor. Left: The graceful facade elegantly expresses its historic past.

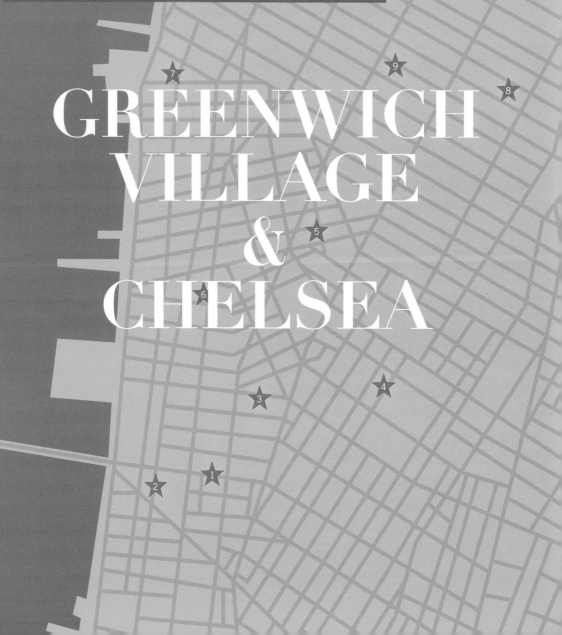

# GREENWICH VILLAGE & CHELSEA

# NEW YORK CITY FIRE MUSEUM

278 Spring Street
(between Hudson
and Varick Streets)
Soho

212.691.1303
www.nycfiremuseum.org

HOURS: Tuesday–Saturday 10 am–5 pm;
Sunday 10 am–4 pm

*I can think of no more stirring symbol of man's humanity to man than a fire engine.*

## Kurt Vonnegut

Fire engines of every description—horse drawn, hand pumped, kerosene powered, and even a vintage motorized engine—can be found at the New York City Fire Museum. This extensive collection includes artifacts from the eighteenth century right up to the present, displayed in a handsome 1904 beaux-arts firehouse still in possession of its original brass sliding pole. Best of all, friendly off-duty firemen are on hand to welcome visitors and tell the story of firefighting in New York City.

It's a wonder that any fires could be controlled during the city's early years, when volunteers had to pull heavy wooden engines through the narrow downtown streets and water was supplied

Above: Ceremonial helmet and fire engine emblem, part of the vast museum collection. Right: Facade of the Fire Museum. Opposite: Photograph of New York City Fire Engine No. 72, in 1915.

Previous page: Detail of 1882 presentation shield. Fire companies often exchanged these as tokens of friendship and esteem.

from a haphazard system of wells and ponds. As the city grew — its population increasing rapidly and new buildings continually under construction—fighting fires became an ever more complex and difficult task.

New York created its first fire department in 1865, replacing volunteers with paid firefighters and finally bringing in horse-drawn engines, which in turn were replaced by mechanized engines. The old telegraph system was converted to alarm boxes; today each firehouse uses an advanced computer dispatch system. As the types of emergencies changed,

the fire department created teams with specialized equipment to handle hazardous materials and formed rescue squads to handle large-scale disasters.

New York City's fire department faced the ultimate challenge on September 11, 2001, when 343 of its firemen died during the terrorist attack on the World Trade Center. The Fire Museum features an exhibition about that tragic day and a moving tribute to all who lost their lives. Those who wore the FDNY uniform became the symbol of heroism to all New Yorkers.

# JOANNE HENDRICKS, COOKBOOKS

The rest of the recipe can be found in *The Alice B. Toklas Cook Book*, where you'll also find the famous recipe for hashish fudge.

These, and hundreds of others, are found in the intriguing collection of antiquarian, out-of-print, and unusual cookbooks at Joanne Hendricks's delightful little bookshop.

Vintage cookbooks, or books about food and wine, appeal to collectors, culinary scholars, and the rest of us searching for a cherished lost recipe, an inspiration for a dinner party, or a specific title by M. F. K. Fisher. This bookstore, so idiosyncratic, has them all: *Larousse Gastronomique, Kippers in Caviar, Il Libro della Polenta, The Japanese Tea Ceremony, Old Warsaw Cookbook,* Tanaquil Le Clercq's *The Ballet Cook Book, Madame Prunier's Fish Cookery Book, Star Trek Cooking Manual,* and A. J. Liebling's *Between Meals.*

Tucked here and there among the books in this tiny space are antique kitchen utensils and cookie cutters, Bennington pottery, nineteenth-century menus, a Victorian beaded tea cosy, vintage Japanese noodle-dipping bowls, and a framed "Paper Plate" by Roy Lichtenstein. Owner Joanne Hendricks says, "There's a story behind the sherry glasses, and tea boxes, and every book."

The bookstore opened in 1995 in this historic brick Federal house. The simple doorway is flanked by Doric columns; the star tie-rods punctuating the facade purposefully keep the bricks from buckling. Built in 1823, the house likely had a shop on the ground floor in the nineteenth century, just as it does today, with its front window full of enticing books.

Above: Facade of the 1823 Federal house, with a front window full of cookbooks.

488 Greenwich Street
(between Spring and Canal Streets)
Greenwich Village,
a block north of Tribeca

212.226.5731
www.joannehendrickscookbooks.com

HOURS: Most days, 11:30 am–6 pm
(Definitely call ahead)

# FILM FORUM

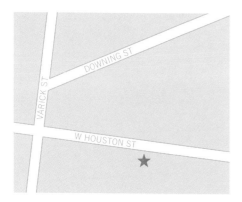

209 West Houston Street
(between Sixth Avenue & Varick Street)
South Village

212.727.8110
www.filmforum.org

HOURS: Open every day;
check the Website for film schedules

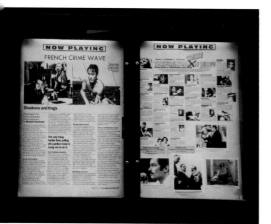

If critics reviewed theaters as well as performances, Film Forum would be ablaze with countless dazzling stars. This much-loved movie house is described by film buffs as a city treasure, a hipster's paradise, a model for cinemas worldwide. They rave about the innovative programming and praise the theater for having the best projection equipment, whether it's screening fragile vintage films or the latest digital productions. They compliment the chocolate egg creams at the concession stand and applaud the piano player who accompanies the silent films. These are passionately loyal fans. One avid admirer has even declared an ambition to be buried there someday: "Up close. Near the screen."

The theater's much-acclaimed programming is structured so

Above: Film schedule on exterior of Film Forum.
Opposite: Theater poster for the French film known in America as *Breathless*. Next page: The glass facade of Film Forum.

Georges de Beauregard présente

JEAN-PAUL BELMONDO          JEAN SEBERG

# A Bout de Souffle

Prix Jean-Vigo 1960

Un Film de
JEAN-LUC GODARD

Scénario Original                    Conseiller Technique
FRANÇOIS TRUFFAUT                    CLAUDE CHABROL

that two distinct yet complementary presentations are running concurrently. Premieres of independent art films are shown on one screen, while a second screen features revivals of classics and directors' retrospectives. For very popular films, a third screen is available for extended runs. It's no wonder that the *New York Times* calls Film Forum "the country's most daring and ambitious presenter… with an influence that reaches far beyond New York City."

Film Forum began in 1970 as an alternative theater for independent films, opening in a small space with a single projector and fifty folding chairs. After three changes of address, the movie house moved to Houston Street in 1989. This modern theater, with its chic glass facade, is as sophisticated and idiosyncratic as the films shown within.

# CENTER FOR ARCHITECTURE

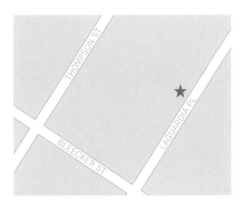

536 LaGuardia Place
(between Bleecker
and West 3rd Streets)
Greenwich Village

212.683.0023
www.aiany.org

HOURS: Monday–Friday 9 am–5 pm

M anhattan has
consistently inspired
in its beholders
*ecstasy about architecture.*

### Rem Koolhaas

Those who are rhapsodic about
modern architecture have a special
affinity for New York's many iconic
contemporary buildings. For true
visionaries intrigued by the idea
of designing for the future, the city's
most essential destination is the
Center for Architecture.

Serving as a museum, resource
center, research facility, and public-
policy forum, the Center is one
of the liveliest places in the design
world. More than a thousand
programs are offered here every
year, open to anyone interested in
innovative architecture and urban
planning.

Exhibitions change frequently
and tend toward the cutting-edge,
drawing enthusiastic crowds. One

recent show explored the daunting problem of creating housing for New York City's expanding population, which is projected to rise in the next few decades from its current 8.2 million to a record 9 million residents. The city's scarcity of available space and high building costs require creative solutions; the Center responded with an exhibition of bold and ingenious proposals.

The Center for Architecture is itself an example of inventive design, with sections of two of its three levels cut away to create a deep, dramatic space filled with natural light. The storefront facade is enticing, with large windows offering a subtle but powerful lure to look inside. It's difficult to walk by without wanting to step in and see an exhibition, listen to a lecture about environmental issues or structural engineering for skyscrapers, or join a discussion about architecturally ambitious projects being planned all over the world, from Brooklyn to Beijing.

Opposite: The ground floor and two basement levels of this building were used to create a 12,000 square-foot space for the Center. Left: View of several levels of the Center for Architecture, with daylight streaming through the front windows.

Previous page: Gallery at the Center for Architecture.

# THREE LIVES
# & COMPANY

Three Lives & Company has been described as a pocket of civility in the city. This small neighborhood bookstore invites people to step inside and share the pleasure of books. It's a literary salon, a hangout, a place where avid readers feel at home. "Ideas and words matter here," as one writer has said.

The place is so welcoming that it's reminiscent of a particular bookshop in Paris that encouraged its customers "to enter with that feeling that they have inherited a book-lined apartment... all the more delightful because they share it with others." Three Lives has the same warm-hearted spirit, which is why so many people feel possessive about this bookstore and why they return, again and again, to find exactly the books they want to read.

This inviting shop is tucked into an 1831 brick building, with a cast-iron pillar standing like a lone bookend at the entrance. Inside, floor-to-ceiling wooden bookshelves and book-filled tables are thronged with a wonderfully chosen collection: all the new titles you have on your list to read, and others you hadn't heard about yet, along with the classics, literature, poetry, travel, and books on New York. Three Lives may be small in size but it has a huge reputation in the literary world. Writers, editors, and publishers all hope to see their books on its front counter—and, even better, talked about here.

Three Lives's name comes from Gertrude Stein's trio of short stories, published in 1909. Perhaps this accounts for the bookstore's literary bent, or perhaps it's because Three Lives is located in the Village, where everything seems to have a literary subtext. The bookshop opened in 1978 and has always appealed to those interested in what another writer calls "real books." The owner, Toby Cox, and everyone who works here is a reader, and, if asked, each has the uncanny ability to know what you'd like to read next—very useful when you're not so sure yourself.

154 West 10th Street
(corner of Waverly Place and 10th Street,
one block east of Seventh Avenue)
Greenwich Village

212.741.2069
www.threelives.com

Above: A favorite corner in Greenwich Village.
Bottom: 1933 edition of *Three Lives* by Gertrude
Stein.

HOURS: Monday–Tuesday 12 pm–8 pm; Wednesday–
Saturday 11 am–8:30 pm; Sunday 12 pm–7 pm

# GARDEN AT ST. LUKE'S IN THE FIELDS

A secret garden lies hidden behind high brick walls in Greenwich Village. This secluded, peaceful place—belonging to the Church of St. Luke's in the Fields—seems far removed from the tumultuous city.

Narrow winding paths circle past the crab apple tree in the center of the garden, leading to benches placed strategically here and there under shady trees. Each season's flora has its admirers: Some garden visitors prefer the ravishing magnolias that announce spring; others love the early June roses or the autumn *Callicarpa americana* and its lavender berries. It may be a surprise to find pomegranates, figs, and rosemary growing here, but the high brick walls miraculously create a microclimate that allows the garden to grow plants rarely seen north of the Carolinas.

A number of Villagers regard this as their private garden, a perfect place for quiet contemplation or reading under a leafy tree. A book by Jane Austen would be appropriate; as one of her characters noted, "To sit in the shade on a fine day, and look upon verdure, is the most perfect refreshment." There's a feeling of being in a country churchyard in an earlier century, when parishioners arrived for services by walking across fields and meadows, or came by boat on the nearby Hudson River.

St. Luke's Church was built in 1821; its elegantly simple architecture is reflected in the row of Federal houses that border the church and share its austere beauty. The garden was begun more than a century later, in 1950, although this is one of those serene places on earth that seems to have been here forever.

ST. LUKE'S CHURCH, HUDSON ST. N.Y.

487 Hudson Street
(Northwest corner of
Hudson and Barrow Streets)
Greenwich Village

HOURS: Open every day 10 am until sunset
Closed on holidays and snow days

Above: Garden of St. Luke's in the Fields.
Opposite: Hand-colored lithograph, 1860.

# THE HIGH LINE

Gansevoort Street to 20th Street
(perched above Washington Street
and Tenth Avenue)
West Village/Chelsea

212.206.9922
www.thehighline.org

HOURS: 7 am-10 pm
(hours may be extended, so check website)

Creating a park in the sky—floating thirty feet above the city streets—is a splendid but improbable idea. Like many successful ventures, this began as a pipe dream: taking a long-abandoned elevated railroad structure built in the 1930s and converting the rusty viaduct into a green space stretching north for a mile and a half, from the West Village through Chelsea.

The design of the High Line incorporates some of the romantic aspects of the original structure. After trains stopped running decades ago, grasses and meadow flowers began to spring up between the tracks. Seeds—dropped by birds or blown by wind—took root

Left: The High Line freight trains ran on elevated tracks between 1934 and the early 1960s, cutting through warehouses and factories. Opposite: A major access point to the High Line is located at the corner of Gansevoort and Washington Streets.

in the gravel ballast and tenaciously flourished. That earlier, self-sown, wild landscape became the inspiration for the new park: A woodland with thick greenery is now planted at Gansevoort Street, water skims a walkway near 15th Street, and grasslands push through the edges of the planked promenade in Chelsea.

Planners of this project cleverly devised a way for visitors to experience the park without hurrying. Entrances lead gradually away from the frenetic streets, hidden niches hold seats perfect for daydreaming, and meandering pathways entice one to linger in this creative sequence of spaces. Every detail has been thought through. The historic art deco steel railings lining the tracks are impeccably restored, using thousands of hand-hammered rivets; the lighting is artfully installed at a low height so that evening ramblers can clearly see the night-time sky.

The first phase of the High Line opened earlier this year, extending from Gansevoort Street to West 20th Street, with the second phase expected to be completed at West 30th Street in several years. Strolling through this spectacular elevated landscape, visitors glimpse unexpected views of the city from a lofty vantage point: a cubist pattern of old and new buildings, streets filled with art galleries, massive nineteenth-century brick warehouses, cobblestone paths in the meatpacking district, piers jutting into the river, towers of skyscrapers in the distance, water taxis and schooners gliding on the Hudson River. Soon, the much-anticipated downtown satellite of the Whitney Museum of American Art will open near the High Line. As the historian Kenneth Jackson has observed, "The juxtaposition of high-density urban development with hardy urban nature is nowhere on earth so stark or so exciting."

Above left:
The railroad tracks
originally stretched
from northern
Manhattan
to Spring Street.
Above right:
Grasses and
meadow flowers
on the abandoned
elevated structure
inspired the
High Line's new
green landscape.
Left Wildflowers
and native
species surround
a walkway of the
High Line.

# IDLEWILD BOOKS

O*ne's destination is never a place, but a new way of seeing things.*

Henry Miller

Idlewild Books is a travel bookstore organized in an original way. Guidebooks are arranged side-by-side with literature, history, travel accounts, and even some cookbooks so that anyone interested in a particular location can approach that place from all angles. More than one hundred countries and all fifty states are represented, with Canada, China, and Cuba each occupying its own regional section on the polished pine bookshelves.

The tall north and south windows create light-filled rooms during the day in this mezzanine space, twelve steps up from the sidewalk. In the evenings, the bookstore often organizes events and readings related to international affairs, travel, and literature in translation.

12 West 19th Street
Chelsea

212.414.8888
www.idlewildbooks.com

HOURS: Monday–Friday 11 am–8 pm;
Saturday and Sunday 12 pm–7 pm

The name of the bookstore was inspired by Idlewild Airport, which served as New York's international airport decades ago, when flying was glamorous. The airport was renamed for John F. Kennedy in 1963, but film buffs remember the last scene in *Breakfast at Tiffany's*, when Holly Golightly tells a taxi driver that she wants to go to Idlewild. Holly would feel right at home in this engaging bookstore.

Opposite: Sun-filled interior at Idlewild Books.

# RUBIN
# MUSEUM OF ART

150 West 17th Street
(corner of Seventh Avenue)
Chelsea

212.620.5000
www.rmanyc.org

HOURS: Monday and Thursday 11 am–5 pm;
Wednesday 11 am–7 pm; Friday 11 am–10 pm;
Saturday and Sunday 11 am–6 pm

The Himalayas may be located far across the world, but some of the region's most spectacular art can be found at the Rubin Museum of Art in Chelsea.

The work may at first seem unfamiliar and mysterious, so the museum wisely encourages visitors to explore the imagery and symbolic language expressed in this outstanding collection. Like all great art, it can be appreciated from many points of view.

Expect to see scenes outside ordinary time, for Himalayan art depicts the extraordinary: vignettes exploding with narrative detail; flying mystics and multiple-headed creatures spinning through space; symbols conveying meaning through gesture, costume, color; demons and deities existing side by side, wrathful or tranquil.

Left: Detail of *Kanakabharadvaja*, from Eastern Tibet. Opposite: A dramatic six-story staircase winds through the interior of the Rubin Museum of Art.

The museum cleverly places magnifying glasses in each gallery to coax visitors to look more closely. Details matter: Surprising discoveries can be made when carefully studying this intricate art.

Part of the pleasure of experiencing the museum's collection is walking up—or down—the dramatic six-story steel and marble staircase that spirals toward a vast skylight, as if climbing to the roof of the world. There are more than 2,000 works in the permanent collection: paintings, sculptures, ritual objects, prints, and textiles dating from the second century to the twenty-first. The museum also organizes some of the most interesting programs in the city: jazz concerts, Tuvan throat singers serenading on 17th Street, Tibetan lotus tea ceremonies, and the favorite Friday night program "CabaretCinema."

The cultural expanse of the Himalayan region is much larger than its geographical area. The Rubin Museum's collection is therefore drawn from the mountain kingdoms of Tibet, Bhutan, Sikkim, and Nepal; westward to Pakistan and Afghanistan; northward to Central Asia, Mongolia, and Siberia; eastward to China; and southward to India and Southeast Asia. The powerful artistic legacy of this huge area is finally beginning to be recognized. To the uninitiated its imagery may be esoteric, but its themes are universal: humanity's place in the universe, wonder at the natural world, remedies for suffering, life after death. As the museum has noted: "Dizzying or serene, transcendent or telling a story, Himalayan art is immediately affecting."

Above: *Vajradhara*, from fourteenth-century Nepal. Opposite: *Amitabha Buddha*, from nineteenth-century central Tibet.

# THE MUSEUM
# AT FIT

Fashion Institute of Technology
Seventh Avenue on the southwest
corner of 27th Street
Chelsea

212.217.4558
www.fitnyc.edu/museum

HOURS: Tuesday–Friday 12 pm–8 pm;
Saturday 10 am–5 pm

*F*ashion is not something
that exists in dresses
only. Fashion is in the
sky, in the street, fashion
has to do with ideas, the way
we live, what is happening.

Coco Chanel

New York is often proclaimed to be
the fashion capital of the world,
so it seems only fitting that there's
a museum in the city dedicated solely
to the art of fashion. This fabulous
place—the Museum at FIT—is best
known for its much-acclaimed
exhibitions and for its vast collection
of clothes and accessories dating
from the eighteenth century to today.

With more than 50,000 items
in the collection, one can imagine
the gargantuan storage space required
to house all of these treasured
objects. Evening gowns designed
by Madame Grès and Isabel Toledo,
Balenciaga and Vivienne Westwood.
Four thousand pairs of shoes. Hats of
every description: bonnets, cloches,

Above: Dresses designed by Isabel Toledo, known for her originality and
technical expertise. Opposite: Evening slippers by Manolo Blahnik, 1988.

Panama straws, snoods, turbans, picture hats. The textile collection is another huge resource, encompassing more than 30,000 items, including 1,300 vintage fabric sample books. Painted textiles created by artists William Morris, Salvador Dali, and Raoul Dufy, among others, inspire the next generation of designers.

The museum, which is part of the highly regarded Fashion Institute of Technology, has been described as a think-tank for fashion studies, offering an ambitious program of lectures, classes, and publications for its diverse audiences. The marvelous exhibitions are always what draw the fashion world—and the rest of us—to come back again and again. Perhaps we like to imagine wearing one of those enchanting creations, just for an evening or two.

Above top: Evening dress designed by Louise Boulanger, 1929. Above left: 1970s wool suit by Mila Schön and owned by Vogue editor Diana Vreeland. Above center: Cloche by Caroline Reboux, 1929. Above right: Suede flats by Christian Louboutin, 1991. Opposite: Alexander McQueen dress made in part from microscope slides dyed red, 2001.

# MIDTOWN MANHATTAN

# SCANDINAVIA HOUSE

The Nordic Center in America
58 Park Avenue (at 38th Street)
Midtown Manhattan

212.879.9779
www.scandinaviahouse.org

HOURS: Tuesday–Saturday 12 pm–6 pm

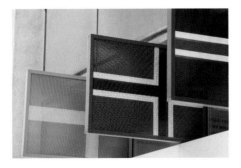

Above: Flags of Scandinavian countries
welcome visitors to this Nordic Center.

**F**lags of five Scandinavian countries—Denmark, Finland, Iceland, Norway, and Sweden—are proudly unfurled at the entrance of this modern, finely detailed building. Scandinavia House, headquarters of the American-Scandinavian Foundation, is well known for its Nordic-themed exhibitions, concerts, film series, lectures, and language courses. Its lively story hours for children feature tales of fierce Viking explorers and hardy sea warriors.

A thousand years ago the Vikings crossed the Atlantic in wooden boats with wind-tight square sails. Archaeological evidence—including the remains of Norse structures—has been discovered in the little fishing village of L'Anse aux Meadows in northern Newfoundland. Not until many centuries later, however, did large numbers migrate from

SCANDINAVIA HOUSE

From Another
Recent Icelandic

Scandinavia to North America. The first to set off, in 1825, were fifty-two Norwegians (plus a baby girl born during the voyage) sailing aboard the tiny sloop *Restauration*; the crossing took fourteen weeks to reach New York.

Nearly two and a half million Scandinavians settled in North America during the nineteenth century. Once here, immigrants sent back letter after letter telling of their life in America and inspiring others to join them. A Swedish journalist visiting America in 1883 wrote that "thousands, millions of such letters (*breflappar*) fell like flakes from a snow cloud over the entire land from Skane to Lapland."

Descendants of these intrepid immigrants, or anyone interested in Nordic history, can spend a fascinating afternoon in the Scandinavia House library, reading books or using its genealogical database to search for long-lost relatives. For those craving still more, a café on the ground floor serves herring and smorgasbord.

---

Above: Detail of Olaus Magnus' map of Scandinavia, 1539. Opposite: The simple elegance of the Scandinavia House facade is reflective of Nordic design aesthetics.

# MAP ROOM
# OF THE NEW YORK
# PUBLIC LIBRARY

Lionel Pincus and Princess Firyal
Map Division, Room 117
Fifth Avenue and 42nd Street
Midtown Manhattan

212.930.0587
www.nypl.org/research/chss/map/
mapping.html

HOURS: Tuesday and Wednesday 1 pm–7:30 pm;
Thursday–Saturday 1 pm–6 pm

Public Library, New York City.

Room 117, known as the Map Room at the New York Public Library, is hardly a secret since it's located in one of the most beloved buildings in the city. Most visitors, though, come to the library to read books or to see the fascinating exhibitions, and are perhaps unaware of its spectacular map collection. Nearly half a million maps can be found here, dating from the sixteenth century to the present day and ranging from the universe of stars and constellations to a single block of Manhattan.

Some of the rarest maps in the world are included in this collection, along with nautical charts, topographic maps, classic engravings, maps of Western expeditions showing frontier routes, property maps that

indicate tax lots, and up-to-date computer-generated maps. More than sixteen thousand atlases and books about cartography are available for research. The Map Room welcomes everyone, including historians, schoolchildren writing reports, archaeologists, map collectors, and preservationists. During World War II, the Army came here to look at maps of Japan; after the attack on the World Trade Center, engineers came to study maps of the downtown infrastructure.

Visitors tend to be particularly interested in maps of New York City, from the 1778 "Plan of the Harbor of New York" to the latest subway maps. It's fascinating to read the history of the city through these visual documents: those from the Dutch era reveal Manhattan's hilly topography; the eight-foot-long Commissioners' Plan of 1811 introduces the city's gridiron street pattern; Viele's Water Map of 1864 describes the streams, marshes, ponds, and original shoreline before landfill expanded the city's boundaries (this map is still used by city engineers today); and contemporary satellite images—taken 517 miles from Earth—clearly show the city's individual buildings, including the New York Public Library.

The Map Room itself is as elegant as the early cartographic specimens in its collection. A recent renovation has brought the space back to its original 1911 splendor, including meticulously gilding the twenty-foot-high beaux-arts ceiling. Sitting in this incredibly beautiful room, with its dramatic corner view of Fifth Avenue and 42nd Street, it's possible to journey to any part of the universe, simply by spending time reading maps in this wide-ranging collection.

Above: Detail of map in the New York Public Library's collection. Opposite: New York map drawn and engraved by M. Rapkin, c. 1850.

Previous page: Left: Vintage postcard of the New York Public Library (the Map Room is located in the right corner of the building). Right: A recent renovation of the Map Room shows the original grandeur of the space.

# CAMPBELL APARTMENT

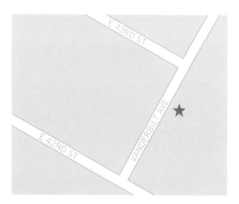

Grand Central Terminal
15 Vanderbilt Avenue entrance
(43rd Street)
Midtown Manhattan

212.953.0409
www.hospitalityholdings.com

HOURS: Monday–Saturday 3 pm–1 am;
Sunday 3 pm–11 pm

**M**ore than half a million people whirl through Grand Central Terminal every day, hurrying with an intensity of motion, rushing to the moment beyond. Few of them know that within the terminal, steps from Vanderbilt Avenue, is a spectacular room designed as a galleried hall of a thirteenth-century Florentine palace. Known today as the Campbell Apartment, this amazing space is open to the public for cocktails from midafternoon until late evening.

The financier John W. Campbell rented this space in 1923 for his office, bringing in a massive Florentine desk, his collection of rare books, a pipe organ, and a Persian rug that was said to be the length of a subway car. The room, which is sixty feet long and thirty feet wide, was further transformed into a palazzo by adding large-scale leaded windows and a vast

stone fireplace and by hand painting the twenty-five-foot-high timbered ceiling.

This was, after all, the decade of the high-living, free-spending 1920s, when a wealthy CEO required a very grand office. Campbell was chairman of his family's firm—Credit Clearing House, which merged with Dun & Bradstreet—and served on the board of the New York Central Railroad.

Campbell and his wife also entertained their friends here, often with concerts in the evening. After his death in 1957, the room was abandoned and became a signalman's office. Happily, in 1999 this remarkable space was restored into an elegant lounge, a welcoming retreat from the frenzy and chaos of the city outside.

Above: Detail of Campbell Apartment's resplendent space. Opposite: Entrance from Vanderbilt Avenue.

# GREENMARKET FARMERS MARKETS

Throughout the city, including
Dag Hammarskjold Plaza at
East 47th Street and Second Avenue
Midtown Manhattan

www.cenyc.org/greenmarket

HOURS: Open Wednesdays year-round
(Check the Website for a schedule
of other farmers markets)

**W**hat's new and unexpected about farmers markets? It's true they've been part of New York for the last three decades, but these markets serve as places of discovery—

or rediscovery—throughout the year. City dwellers look forward to what the changing seasons will bring, knowing that spring has arrived when asparagus and rhubarb appear, just as the first apples of the season—Paula Reds and Macouns—announce the approach of September.

Everything sold at the open-air farmers markets is grown, foraged, caught, or raised within a 250-mile radius of New York City: farmstead cheeses, fresh-caught ocean fish, artisanal wines and ciders, livestock raised in local pastures, homemade

Farmers Markets have been a tradition in the city for three decades.

jams and breads, honey from a farm beehive, maple syrup tapped from rural trees, and every imaginable assortment of fruits and vegetables, including more than one hundred varieties of tomatoes.

Greenmarket began in 1976, when twelve farmers set up stalls in an empty lot in Manhattan and started selling their homegrown crops. The initiative had a two-part mission: to provide fresh, locally grown produce to New Yorkers while helping small regional farms stay in business. What began as a modest venture has now become an enterprising network of farmers markets located at nearly fifty sites all over the city. Union Square Greenmarket is the superstar, open four days every week year-round, although the other markets are open one day or two each week.

Urban ramblers often turn a corner and find an unexpected Greenmarket: under the trees in Abingdon Square in Greenwich Village, in Poe Park on the Grand Concourse in the Bronx, at Grand Army Plaza at the edge of Brooklyn's Prospect Park, inside the Staten Island ferry terminal in lower Manhattan, at Tucker Square across from Lincoln Center. The photographs on these pages were taken at the Dag Hammarskjold

If farmers markets have whetted your interest in farms, go directly to the Queens County Farm Museum and spend a day roaming its forty-seven acres. This is the last remaining tract of farmland in the city; the museum offers year-round events for children, including hayrides every day, weather permitting. Call 718.347.3276 or visit the website: www.queensfarm.org

Plaza farmers market, a block away from the United Nations. Each of these places evokes the markets that existed in New York City in the past—from the fabled Washington Market demolished in the 1960s, all the way back to the Dutch marketplace selling corn and fish near Fort Amsterdam in the seventeenth century.

# JAPAN SOCIETY

333 East 47th Street
(between First and Second Avenues)
Midtown Manhattan

212.832.1155
www.japansociety.org

HOURS: Tuesday–Thursday 11 am–6 pm; Friday
11 am–9 pm; Saturday and Sunday 11 am–5 pm

Above: Advertisement for Society-sponsored
trips to Japan, c. 1913.

**J**apan comprises more than three thousand islands extending along the Pacific coast of Asia. Far across the world in New York, the serene and elegant home of the Japan Society can be thought of as another island, perfectly capturing the spirit of this East Asian country.

The building's architect, Junzo Yoshimura, designed the interior spaces to open onto the gardens to "create a harmonious whole." Nature is always a significant element in Japanese gardens, as it is here—particularly the use of water. Visitors to the Japan Society will discover a bamboo pool, a meandering stream, and a waterfall and perhaps think of the haiku written by the seventeenth-century poet Matsuo Basho: *Petals of the mountain rose / fall now and then / to the roar of the waterfall.*

The Japan Society has existed in New York for more than a century. It was founded in 1907 to foster strong cultural ties between the United States and Japan, as well as to create a dialogue on issues important to both

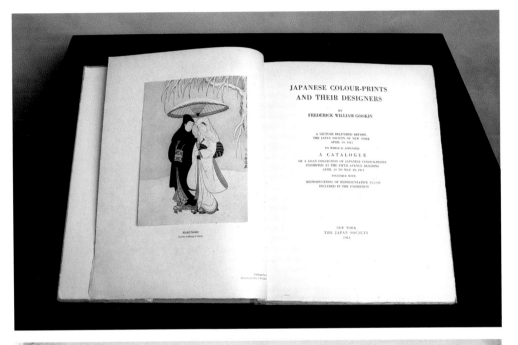

Above top: Japan Society's tradition of publishing and exhibiting has created wide interest in Japanese culture. Above: Invitation to a Japan Society dinner in 1910. Opposite: Colorful banners at the entrance.

countries. During the earliest years, a lecture series was started, books were published, and an exhibition of *ukiyo-e* prints was seen by some 8,000 New Yorkers.

These activities set a pattern for the future; today, the Japan Society presents more than one hundred events each year. The art gallery, library, auditorium, and classrooms draw visitors interested in its film series, which ranges from Kurosawa to Tora-san, or its lectures on Japanese folk art, robotic technology, or the ancient musical instruments known as *gagaku*. Education programs include haiku workshops, language classes, and a course on calligraphy; its acclaimed performing arts offers wide-ranging presentations, from traditional comedy known as *rakugo* to experimental new music to classic Noh repertoire.

Many visitors come especially to see the Society's renowned exhibitions. These have included Zen figure painting in medieval Japan, a retrospective of Yoko Ono's work, Japanese bamboo as a sculptural medium, and the finest contemporary Japanese ceramic artists. Reviewing one show—which could describe any at the Japan Society—the *New York Times* wrote: "You really feel you've been somewhere out of the ordinary. And you have."

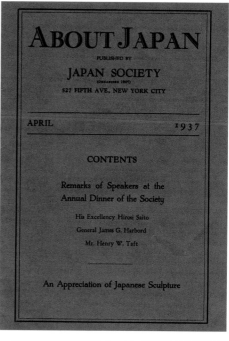

Above top: The Japan Society has published books since its earliest years. Above: View of the indoor bamboo garden and waterfall.

# CHAPEL OF THE GOOD SHEPHERD

The Erol Beker Chapel at
St. Peter's Church
619 Lexington Avenue
(Enter at 54th Street)
Midtown Manhattan

212.935.2200
www.saintpeters.org

HOURS: Call ahead

**T**his tiny chapel is one of the most subtle and original spaces in New York. Designed by the legendary sculptor Louise Nevelson, the chapel perfectly captures her wish to create "a place of purity."

The asymmetrical, five-sided white walls of the chapel are a background for Nevelson's extraordinary white-painted wood sculptures. The intimacy of the space, the imagery evoked in the sculptures, the light from the white frosted window, all convey a feeling of tranquility. Nevelson designed every detail: the gold-leafed Cross of the Good Shepherd over the altar, vestments for the clergy, and the three suspended columns swaying slightly in the air currents.

Left: Detail of the Chapel of the Good Shepherd's sculptural space.

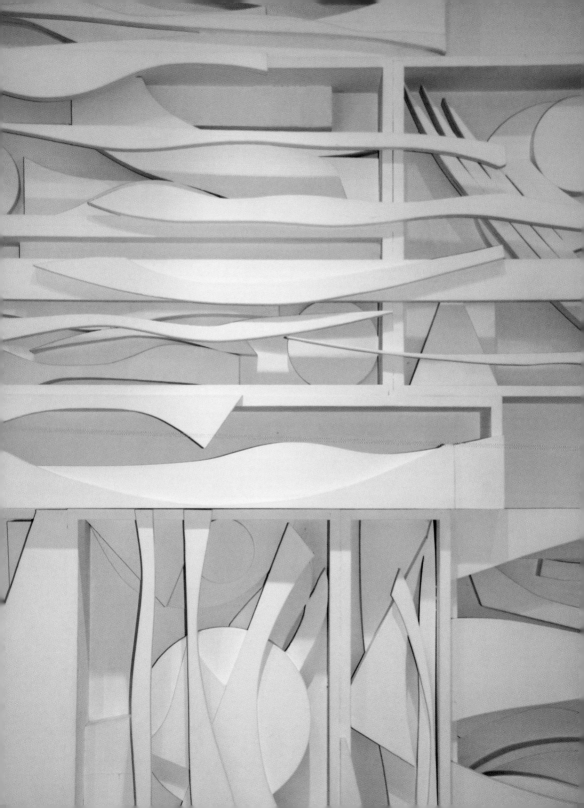

Louise Nevelson was born in Russia in 1899 and came to America as a young girl. She tenaciously exhibited her art for decades before achieving success, although she had long been renowned for her sculpture by the time she created the Chapel of the Good Shepherd in 1977. Intensely subjective and intuitive in her approach to art, Nevelson liked to say that "Picasso resolved the cube, Mondrian flattened it, and I embraced it with poetry."

The Chapel of the Good Shepherd, so fitting a place for meditation or prayer or a half-hour of quiet thoughts, is open to visitors.

Above top: The five-sided space of the small chapel measures twenty-eight by twenty-one feet. Above: Louise Nevelson was celebrated with a commemorative U. S. postage stamp in 2000. Opposite: Detail of the sculpture on the east wall, titled *Frieze of the Apostles.*

# THE GROLIER CLUB

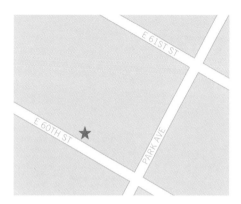

47 East 60th Street
(between Madison and Park Avenues)
Midtown Manhattan

212.838.6690
www.grolierclub.org

HOURS: Monday–Saturday 10 am–5 pm
Closed during August

Left: The
Grolier Club
has published
over two
hundred books
and exhibition
catalogues.
Opposite:
Exhibitions
are open to the
public in
this Grolier
Club Gallery.

T he Grolier is a distinguished club for book lovers — or bibliophiles, as they would say — who perfectly understand Thomas Jefferson's assertion: "I cannot live without books."

Founded in 1884, the Grolier was one of the first organizations in America to regard books and prints as objects worthy of display, comparable with painting and sculpture. The club has presented more than five hundred exhibitions over the years — all open to the public free of charge. Four are organized each year in the main gallery, with themes ranging from polar explorations (in a display titled "Books on Ice") to a recent show celebrating the five hundredth anniversary of Henry VIII's accession.

Other exhibitions have featured Virginia Woolf, the type designer and calligrapher Hermann Zapf, the Eragny Press, Marcel Proust, woodcuts in early printed books,

Whistler in Venice, modern fine presses, books of Cuban artists, Dr. Samuel Johnson, and 4,000 years of miniature books. Personal libraries are also shown, including Jorge Luis Borges's books and manuscripts from Buenos Aires and Georgia O'Keeffe's books and ephemera from her adobe house in Abiquiu, New Mexico. Several decades ago, an exhibition demurely titled "Mementos" included Voltaire's red briefcase, Robert Browning's blotting paper, Gertrude Stein's vest, and Wordsworth's spectacles, among other memorable objects.

The Grolier has more than seven hundred members, all of whom are involved in various bookish pursuits as writers, scholars, collectors, librarians, printers, and publishers. Its library has a collection of more than 100,000 books about books, from illuminated manuscripts to volumes created by modern presses. This remarkable library may be visited by appointment, an opportunity that delights the many researchers intrigued by its huge number of book-auction and bookseller catalogues dating back to the seventeenth century.

Located in a six-story 1917 neo-Georgian townhouse, the Grolier Club is named after the great French bibliophile Jean Grolier (1489–1565), who was renowned for sharing his library with friends.

# TENDER BUTTONS

143 East 62nd Street
(Between Lexington and
Third Avenues)
Midtown Manhattan

212.758.7004

HOURS: Monday–Friday 10:30 am–6 pm;
Saturday 10:30 am–5:30 pm

**D**o you remember the children's game Button, Button, Who's Got the Button? If the question is, rather, who's got the really fabulous buttons, the memorable buttons, the ones that capture your heart, then the answer is definitely Tender Buttons, a tiny shop with a vast selection. Since 1967, this beguiling place has specialized in unique and interesting buttons that are nestled in boxes lining a wall from floor to ceiling or—for some of the rarest—framed as works of art.

Many of their buttons are vintage, created in gold, faceted glass, French amber, inlaid wood, Bakelite, precious stones, pearl, Navajo silver, scrimshaw, and every material imaginable. Some are designed as rosebuds or miniature cigarette packs or American eagles. There are diamond-shaped silver buttons for Scottish kilts and spherical brass buttons from Civil War uniforms. A set of three cocktail buttons from

the 1930s—a martini, a Manhattan, and a Side Car—celebrates the repeal of Prohibition. Exquisite portraits are painted on nineteenth-century buttons made of French ivory or Japanese Satsuma porcelain.

Buttons have a long history; they've even been found by archaeologists in prehistoric sites. Crusaders are thought to have introduced the buttonhole to Europe from the Middle East, which certainly made buttons functional as well as decorative. Over the centuries they've been used "to flaunt wealth, mourn loved ones, smuggle secrets, and stop bullets," as a button historian has noted. Step into Tender Buttons and ruminate about the unpredictable history of these small wonders.

Above and opposite: Details of delightful Tender Buttons.

# UPPER MANHATTAN & THE BRONX

# NICHOLAS ROERICH MUSEUM

319 West 107th Street at Riverside Drive
Upper Manhattan

212.864.7752
www.roerich.org

HOURS: Tuesday–Sunday 2 pm–5 pm

**A**n astonishing collection of art can be found in this small museum, which houses more than two hundred paintings by Nicholas Roerich.

Step inside the 1898 townhouse and enter the world of a prolific artist who was also an idealist, philosopher, teacher, and statesman.

Roerich's earliest paintings express his fascination with Russia's past—its legends and saints, churches and castles. He is best known for his later paintings, created after he had embarked on a series of expeditions to the remote mountain ranges of the Himalayas. These paintings, so passionate and intense, celebrate the towering mountains and spiritual values he found when living in the East.

As with his art, there are many facets to Nicholas Roerich. He was born in St. Petersburg, Russia, in 1874 into a well-to-do family. As a

young man, he made a name for himself in Paris by creating sets and costumes for Diaghilev's avant-garde productions. He first came to America in 1920 for a New York exhibition of his paintings and returned frequently between his world travels. Roerich died in 1947 at his home in the Himalayan foothills.

One of his greatest accomplishments was the Roerich Pact, a treaty designed to protect cultural treasures even during times of war; it was signed at the White House by thirty-six nations in 1935. The symbol of the Roerich Pact was the Banner of Peace, unfurled today outside the museum. Its design shows three magenta circles surrounded by a large sphere. Like much of Roerich's work, its meaning has a number of interpretations: The circles may be a unity of art, religion, and science or may represent the past, present, and future, surrounded by eternity.

Above: Painting by Nicholas Roerich, titled *Old Pskov*, 1922. Opposite: Exterior of the 1898 townhouse housing the Nicholas Roerich Museum.

Previous page: Portrait of Nicholas Roerich in India, c. 1931.

# THE BIBLICAL GARDEN

at the Cathedral Church of
St. John the Divine
Amsterdam Avenue and 112th Street
Upper Manhattan

212.316.7540
www.stjohndivine.org

HOURS: Open every day during daylight hours

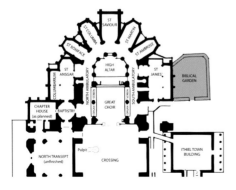

A small, green sanctuary hidden from the street, the Biblical Garden is located near the southeast end of the Cathedral Church of St. John the Divine.

Every plant that has been chosen is mentioned in the Bible. Boxwood hedges embrace plantings of quince, plum, laurel, iris, and lilies. Roses climb Gothic arches. Tall junipers reach toward the sky like the spires of the nearby cathedral.

The garden is best described by the poet Gerald Stern:

> *A biblical fantasy of trees and*
> *   herbs and flowers*
> *from Matthew and John and*
> *   Samuel, laid out in perfect*
> *clusters, poplar from Genesis,*
> *   reeds from Kings,*
> *nettles from Job, lovely carob*
> *   from Luke*

This little horticultural gem is shaded by the stone walls of the Cathedral Church of St. John the Divine, one of the glories of Christendom. Construction of the cathedral began in 1892, and the work of finishing it continues today. Originally designed in a Romanesque Byzantine style by the architects Heins and LaFarge, the plans were revised two decades later by the architect Ralph Adams Cram, who changed course and chose a Gothic-revival design instead.

The transition between the two styles—from Romanesque to Gothic—has created an extraordinary building. The new design lengthened the nave to 601 feet and expanded the traditional three aisles to five, making the cathedral unlike any other on earth. Everything about St. John the Divine is monumental: The vaulted ceiling soars 124 feet; the exquisite rose window is composed of 10,000 pieces of glass; the Aeolian-Skinner organ is equipped with 8,035 pipes.

Even the much-loved seven chapels, dedicated to the patron saints of the city's major immigrant groups, are called "little churches," with space for 150 worshipers in each. The cathedral itself can accommodate five thousand people; on the annual day of the Blessing of the Animals in autumn, household pets—and often an elephant or camel—join the congregation.

The cathedral's most famous creatures, though, can be found in the Biblical Garden. Beautiful, proud peacocks stroll through the paths and into the church grounds, trailing their iridescent blue-green tail feathers and then suddenly stopping to display their extravagant plumage, as if in exaltation—their way of saying *Gloria in excelsis Deo.*

Above: One of the colorful peacocks on the Cathedral grounds. Opposite: A meandering path through the exquisite Biblical Garden.

Previous page: Detail of floor plan of Cathedral Church of St. John the Divine. Rght: View of the east side of the Cathedral from the Biblical Garden.

# THE HISPANIC SOCIETY OF AMERICA

Audubon Terrace
Broadway, between 155th
and 156th Streets
Upper Manhattan

212.926.2234
www.hispanicsociety.org

HOURS: Tuesday–Saturday 10 am–4:30 pm;
Sunday 1 pm–4 pm

This impressive collection of Hispanic art and literature is an unexpected discovery. Secluded in the northern reaches of Manhattan yet only steps from a subway station at 157th Street (on the #1 line), the Hispanic Society of America surprises visitors with its grand building and splendid interior spaces. The red terracotta archways within the main court form a dramatic background for the museum's remarkable art.

The Hispanic collection was assembled by Archer Milton Huntington, heir to a great railroad fortune, who dreamed of creating a great museum. He began by acquiring rare books and manuscripts and then added sculpture and decorative arts. All are now part of the Hispanic

Left: Facade of the Hispanic Society of America.
Opposite: Goya's famous 1797 painting,
*The Duchess of Alba*.

124

Society, including an intricately carved ivory box from the tenth century, letters from Philip II, silk textiles from Islamic Spain, medieval charters, sixteenth-century gold and silver from Latin América, and first editions of *Don Quixote*.

The collection comprises more than eight hundred paintings, as well as watercolors and drawings, dating from the medieval period to the early twentieth century. Many visitors come specifically to see the three portraits by Diego Velázquez, the *Holy Family* by El Greco, works by the seventeenth-century masters Francisco de Zurbarán, José de Ribera, and Bartolomé Estéban Murillo—and, above all, the paintings and etchings created by Francisco de Goya.

*The Duchess of Alba*, painted by Goya in 1797, is the best-known painting in the collection and perhaps the best-loved, too. In the portrait the duchess is dressed in black—she'd been recently widowed at the age of thirty-five—and enigmatically points to the ground, where the words "solo Goya" are written. One of her rings is also inscribed with the artist's name. There has been much speculation about the relationship between Goya and the Duchess of Alba, although this mystery remains

unsolved. The duchess was without doubt very alluring, as noted by a visitor to Spain at the time who commented that "every hair on her head elicits desire."

The Hispanic Society of America was founded in 1904 by Huntington, who built a group of classical buildings on what was originally the Audubon estate and game preserve. The formal beaux-arts structures housed a number of museums that have since moved away. There's talk that the Hispanic Society may also venture downtown, but many New Yorkers hope that it will remain in this spectacular space at Audubon Terrace.

Above: Detail from the upper level, with displays of decorative arts. Opposite: The two-story high Main Court, with ornately decorated terracotta archways.

127

# GARDENS OF THE CLOISTERS

Fort Tryon Park
Northern Manhattan

212.923.3700
www.metmuseum.org/cloisters

HOURS: (March–October) Tuesday–Sunday
9:30 am–5:15 pm; (November–February)
Tuesday–Sunday 9:30 am–4:45 pm

The Unicorn Tapestries entice scores of visitors to the Cloisters, but the gardens have their own admirers. These three gardens, planted in reconstructed Romanesque and Gothic cloisters, provide a place for contemplation and tranquil thoughts, far away from the whirlwind of the city.

Inspired by medieval paintings and tapestries, the gardens give us an appreciation for life in the Middle Ages. The Cuxa Cloister contains the Garth Garden, designed in a typical medieval plan, with a fountain set on the axis of four paths that divide the garden into quadrants. The bright fragrant flowers bordering the paths and the crab apple trees within the quadrants make the strict symmetry of the space seem joyful rather than austere.

Left: The Garth Garden in the Cuxa Cloister.
Opposite: Detail of the Bonnefont Cloister.

The Herb Garden in the Bonne-font Cloister is based on the four-hundred species of plants known in the Middle Ages. Raised beds and wattled fences are used here, just as they were in medieval times. Plants are carefully labeled, listing the variety of ways in which herbs were used in households of the day—for cooking and medical purposes, making perfumes and dyes, and even for mixing magic potions.

The Trie Cloister Garden contains plants depicted in the unicorn tapestries. Planted as a single field of blooms, the garden resembles the thousand flowers, *les millefleurs,* depicted in medieval tapestries. All three gardens

were created in 1938, when the Cloisters opened as a branch of the Metropolitan Museum of Art.

And how did it happen that the Cloisters and its splendid gardens are in northern Manhattan? The generosity of John D. Rockefeller Jr. created this extraordinary place. He purchased the land that became Fort Tryon Park and built the Cloisters at its highest point. He then acquired the collection of medieval art and architecture that had been amassed by George Gray Barnard (nearly seven hundred pieces, including large sections of the cloisters of four medieval monasteries), and donated his own Gothic sculptures and fifteenth-century tapestries. Rockefeller also helped to preserve the sheer cliffs of the Palisades across the river, to protect the Cloister's glorious views forever.

Above: Detail of column in the Cuxa Cloister.
Opposite: The Garth Garden; in a medieval
monastic complex, an open-air yard
enclosed by cloisters was known as a garth.

*From a place in the
kingdom of France
they brought the stained
glass and the stones
to build on the island
of Manhattan
these concave cloisters.*

Jorge Luis Borges

# DYCKMAN FARMHOUSE

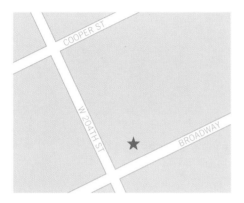

4881 Broadway (at 204th Street)
Upper Manhattan

212.304.9422
www.dyckmanfarmhouse.org

HOURS: Wednesday–Saturday 11 am–4 pm;
Sunday 12 pm–4 pm

Above: The half-timbered wood hut, known
as the Hessian Hut, in the garden of Dyckman
Farmhouse. Opposite: The eighteenth-
century Dyckman Farmhouse sits high above
Broadway.

The eighteenth-century Dyckman Farmhouse, a small, endearing museum, was once part of a huge property of 250 acres stretching across Manhattan east to west, from river to river.

Today, the farmhouse is closely surrounded by the city and all its intrusive clamor. Yet, once inside the house, or sitting on the tranquil back porch overlooking the garden, visitors experience the delightful illusion of stepping far back in time.

In 1776, during the Revolutionary War, William Dyckman—grandson of Jan, the first Dyckman to settle in this area—fled with his family when British troops occupied Manhattan. When the war ended, they returned to find their home and much of the property destroyed. William replanted the land and constructed a new home for the family around 1784—and this is the house we see

today. Typically Dutch colonial in style, it was built with a pitched gambrel roof, eaves that sheltered wide porches on two sides of the structure, and an elegant brick facade; fieldstone and white-painted clapboard were used for the rest of the house.

The Dyckmans lived here for three generations. They furnished their home with four-poster beds, portraits of the family, and early American parlor furniture. Like many farmhouses of the era, there was a summer kitchen in an adjacent wing and a winter kitchen in the basement, keeping the house warm during the cold months. The latter must have been the coziest space in the house, with its low-beamed ceiling and its wide hearth fitted with cookware; it's still a welcoming room, evoking fond memories of family meals prepared here.

Eventually, in the 1870s, the house was sold. As the decades passed, the area changed rapidly from a rural community to an urban neighborhood until even the little farmhouse was threatened with demolition. In 1915, Mary Alice Dyckman Dean and Fannie Frederica Dyckman Welch, daughters of the last Dyckman to grow up in the house, purchased the property and restored it. The next year they gave this much-loved historic house to the city. Today, the Dyckman Farmhouse Museum teaches us about early American life while "preserving the past for future generations." The museum is also known for its summer concerts in the garden and exhibitions in the parlors, along with lively educational tours for schoolchildren.

The commanding view of rivers and hills has disappeared, along with the apple orchards and cider mill once part of the farm. The Hessian soldiers who camped in its garden during the Revolutionary War are now just a legend, and deer no longer roam the land. Yet a red-tailed hawk still comes to visit, flying through the garden, as a reminder that Manhattan was once a wilderness.

Above: Lithograph of the farmhouse, 1866. Opposite: The wide porches of Dyckman Farmhouse seem far away from the city's clamor.

# WAVE HILL

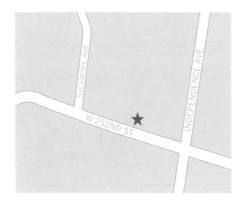

675 West 252nd Street
Riverdale, Bronx

718.549.3200
www.wavehill.org

HOURS: (April 15–October 14)
Tuesday–Sunday 9 am–5:30 pm;
(October 15–April 14)
Tuesday–Sunday 9 am–4:30 pm

ave Hill is a small paradise located at the edge of the city, overlooking the Hudson River and Palisades. Its twenty-eight acres of gardens and woodlands create a place of ethereal beauty—so secluded and tranquil that a visit here is like spending a day in the country.

The first view one sees is a dramatic introduction to Wave Hill: a perspective that leads the way across a spacious lawn toward a stone terrace and its elegant pergola, which perfectly frames the river and sheer cliffs beyond. Serious horticulturalists march straight to the gardens and greenhouses, since even the most knowledgeable delight in finding the unexpected here.

Visitors amble about, admiring the mixture of vintage and modern perennials in the lovely Flower Garden and enjoying the exuberant effect of the pastoral Wild Garden. There are so many exquisite gardens to see here:

Left: Water lily floating in the pool at the Aquatic Garden. Opposite: Upper pergola supporting a collection of cascading vines.

the vertical Alpine Garden cascading down a rustic wall, the Herb Garden tucked between bluestone paths, the formal Aquatic Garden with its tropical water plants and grasses, and the adjacent Monocot Garden, sensuous in texture and form.

And the trees! The spectacular trees at Wave Hill—some of which were planted more than a century ago—create an imposing background for the ever-changing gardens. The arboreal collection includes American elm, sugar maple, sumac, beech, sequoia, and a dozen other species. Undaunted walkers can see even more specimens on the Woodland Trail winding through ten acres on the outer edges of the grounds. For those who would rather sit under the trees, there are comfortable straight-back chairs inspired by the iconic Gerrit Rietveld design—ideal for reading or daydreaming or admiring the landscape.

Wave Hill is also a cultural center, with exhibitions, seasonal performing arts, and programs in horticulture, woodland management, and environmental education. Originally a country home, and before that farmland, it is the only Hudson River estate that is located within the city today. A succession of owners improved the land—particularly George W. Perkins, the last owner, who purchased the house in 1903. His landscape designs included contouring the land, planting rare trees, and creating innovative gardens, all of which complemented the property's magnificent vistas. In 1960, his family deeded Wave Hill to the City of New York.

The roster of illustrious people who have lived at Wave Hill is long. Teddy Roosevelt's parents rented the property for two summers—in 1870 and 1871—when Teddy was eleven and twelve years old. Legend has it that he first became interested in conservation here, which may or may not be true, although it's certainly easy to imagine him climbing a copper beech tree or rambling through these woods. Over the years, other interesting tenants have included Mark Twain, who set up a tree-house parlor in the branches of a chestnut tree on the lawn; the acclaimed maestro Arturo Toscanini; the British ambassador to the United Nations; and—not least—Bashford Dean, curator of arms and armor at the Metropolitan Museum of Art as well as curator of reptiles and fish at the American Museum of Natural History, posts that he held *simultaneously*.

# SCHOMBURG CENTER FOR RESEARCH IN BLACK CULTURE

515 Malcolm X Boulevard
(at 135th Street)
Harlem

212.491.2200
www.schomburgcenter.org

HOURS: Tuesday–Wednesday 12 pm–8 pm;
Thursday and Friday 12 pm–10 pm;
Saturday 10 am–6 pm

*I've known rivers:*
*Ancient, dusky rivers.*
*My soul has grown deep like the rivers.*

Langston Hughes

A collection of more than ten million items can be found at the Schomburg Center, one of the world's largest and most comprehensive libraries for the study of black culture.

Among the treasures are Civil War documents, church records, family letters and scrapbooks, African grammars, an official report of a raid in 1724, ledgers from the Audubon Ballroom, a collection of papers from the West Indies, a remarkable photography collection, and the archives of Booker T. Washington.

An impressive file of African American newspapers dating back to the early nineteenth century is housed here, as well as Howard Orphanage records, F.B.I. files on the Black Panthers, an 1819 agricultural report from Antigua, and theater

**Books ARE WEAPONS**

READ ABOUT...

THE NEGRO IN NATIONAL DEFENSE
AFRICA AND THE WAR
NEGRO HISTORY AND CULTURE

J.P.

AT THE SCHOMBURG COLLECTION OF THE
**NEW YORK PUBLIC LIBRARY**
104 WEST 136th STREET NEW YORK CITY

his home until the collection was acquired by the New York Public Library and moved to its 135th Street branch in 1926; Schomburg then became curator of the collection.

That small branch library evolved into what is today an enormous research library. The original structure at 103 West 135th Street—built in 1905 in the style of an Italian palazzo—is now part of the Schomburg Center and used as an exhibition space. This was the famous gathering place for writers and artists of the Harlem Renaissance during the 1920s. Innumerable lectures, poetry readings, plays, art exhibitions, and political discussions have made this site a magnet for the neighborhood—then and now.

The acclaimed poet Langston Hughes is one of the writers closely connected to the Schomburg Center. He had come to New York from Missouri to study at Columbia University and lived down the street from the library, at the 135th Street YMCA. Known as "the Negro Poet Laureate," Hughes achieved great literary success in his life. He created a vast quantity of remarkable poetry, eleven plays, and countless works of prose. When he died in 1967, his ashes were interred at the Schomburg Center beneath a terrazzo cosmogram inspired by his poem "The Negro Speaks of Rivers."

scripts given by Ossie Davis and Ruby Dee. The papers of the Civil Rights Congress are here, as are those of Richard Wright, Claude McKay, Mabel Mercer, Paul Robeson, Ralph Bunche, Arthur Ashe, Alex Haley, Lena Horne, and A. Philip Randolph.

This amazing collection was begun by Arthur A. Schomburg, a book dealer and historian, who amassed books, newspapers, photographs, and anything he could find that documented the black experience. He kept everything in

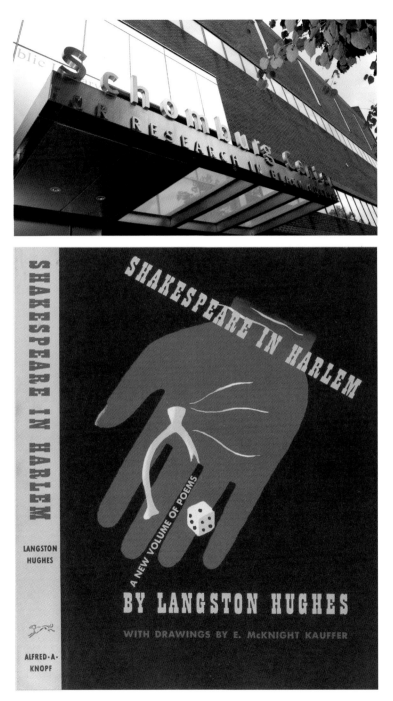

# MUSEUM OF THE CITY OF NEW YORK

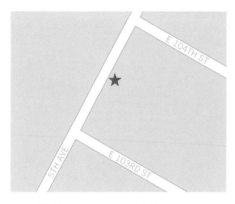

1220 Fifth Avenue at 103rd Street
Upper Manhattan

212.534.1672
www.mcny.org

HOURS: Tuesday–Sunday 10 am–5 pm

The photography collection at the Museum of the City of New York (MCNY) is one of the city's great treasures. This enormous collection, with more than 500,000 images, shows the unique and irresistible visual power of New York. Wide-angled or intimate, oblique or close-up, the photographs remind us that this is a city both constant yet forever changing.

The photo to the left is titled "Chicago to New York Auto Race, c. 1913," from the Byron Collection. The immediacy of this image is striking: The race is about to begin, the car ready to bolt, and the spectators in jaunty hats stand by, perhaps envying the driver. The photograph opposite, taken by Samuel H. Gottscho in 1932, depicts a person half-hidden among

Left: *Chicago to New York Auto Race*, c. 1913, photograph from the Byron Collection. Opposite: *View of the Financial District*, photographed by Samuel H. Gottscho, 1932.

abstract shapes: buildings formed in squares and towering rectangles, cars parked in a crisscross of light and shadow, an elevated railway track swooping across the image like a black streak. Looking at these photos today, time becomes visible.

MCNY's photographs range from some of the earliest views of New York, depicted in the mid-nineteenth-century waxed-paper negatives of Victor Prevost, to contemporary photos of the city by Joel Meyerowitz. The collection includes the photographic archives of the Byron Company, Irving Underhill, the Gottscho-Schleisner firm, *LOOK* magazine, Charles Von Urban, and the Wurts Brothers. All of the notable New York photographers are represented here, including Jacob Riis, Jessie Tarbox Beals, Bruce Davidson, and of course Berenice Abbott, the quintessential photographer of New York, whose famous 1939 series of city portraits were originally sponsored by MCNY.

It's often said that photographs are "ways of seeing." Viewers can see the shape of the city—the dreams of the city—during photo exhibitions at MCNY. Recent shows have presented iconic views by Rudy Burckhardt, evocative portraits by Carl Van Vechten, bold images of New York taken by the unknown master Eugene de Salignac, new perspectives by contemporary Dutch photographers, and haunting photos of the South Bronx by Ray Mortenson.

The photographs are wonderful, and so is the rest of the museum. Visitors like to hopscotch through, stopping to see an exhibition, hear an engrossing lecture, or drop by the theater collection. Children invariably insist on revisiting the ship models or the famous Stettenheimer dollhouse. In many ways, MCNY is more than a museum, since New Yorkers also like to think of this appealing place as a dear friend: a lively, thought-provoking, engaging friend whom you've known forever, and yet who never fails to be fascinating.

Above: *Greyhound Bus Terminal*, photographed by Berenice Abbott, 1936. Opposite: Detail of *Harlem Street II*, photographed by Berenice Abbott, 1938.

# NEW YORK ACADEMY OF MEDICINE

1216 Fifth Avenue (at 103rd Street)
Upper Manhattan

212.822.7315 (Library)
212.822.7310 (Historical Collection)

HOURS: Library open Monday–Friday 9 am–5 pm;
Wednesday until 7 pm
Visits by appointment only.

Above and opposite: German medical chart,
c. 1903.

The Library at the New York Academy of Medicine has one of the great medical collections in the world, with more than 800,000 books, although few people outside the world of medicine seem to know about this distinguished place. Open to the public by appointment, the library's holdings are so vast that if extended end to end, they would stretch for over fourteen miles—longer even than the island of Manhattan, whose narrow length surprisingly unfolds to only 13.4 miles.

Visitors may pore over medical volumes in the main reading room, a civilized space in which you may find yourself sitting next to a physician or a scientist. The main collection emphasizes biomedical literature that is primarily clinical in nature; there are also extensive holdings in books on bioethics, public policy, and the

# Skelett des Menschen I.

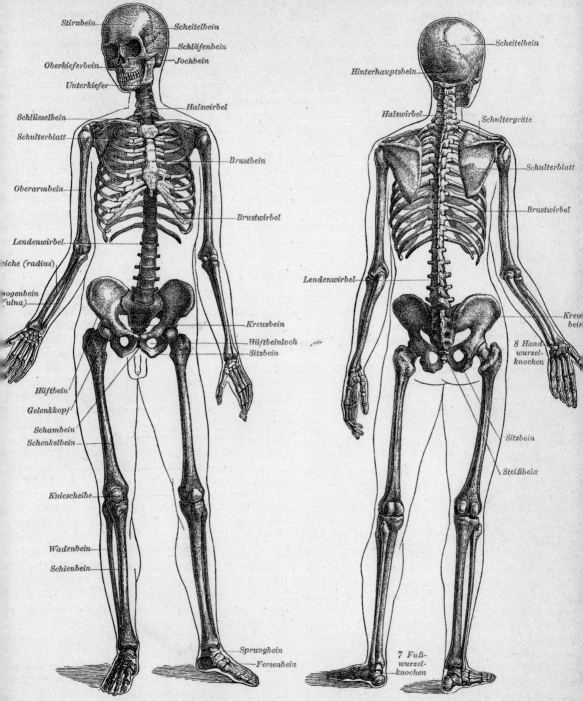

**Skelett von vorn (linke Figur):**
Stirnbein, Scheitelbein, Schläfenbein, Jochbein, Oberkieferbein, Unterkiefer, Halswirbel, Schlüsselbein, Schulterblatt, Brustbein, Oberarmbein, Brustwirbel, Lendenwirbel, ...iche (radius), ...ogenbein (ulna), Kreuzbein, Hüftbeinloch, Sitzbein, Hüftbein, Gelenkkopf, Schambein, Schenkelbein, Kniescheibe, Wadenbein, Schienbein, Sprungbein, Fersenbein

**Skelett von hinten (rechte Figur):**
Scheitelbein, Hinterhauptsbein, Halswirbel, Schultergräte, Schulterblatt, Brustwirbel, Lendenwirbel, Kreuzbein, 8 Handwurzelknochen, Sitzbein, Steißbein, 7 Fußwurzelknochen

1. Skelett von vorn.   2. Skelett von hinten.

history of medicine. The library keeps up-to-date with about a thousand current medical journals.

For visitors interested in the library's extraordinary rare-book collection, this too may be visited by appointment. More than 50,000 books, manuscripts, and artifacts can be found here, including an Egyptian papyrus describing surgery, written in 1700 B.C.; a spine-chilling metal amputation set from 1820, nestled in a wooden box lined in velvet; an amusing series of 300-plus pharmaceutical trade cards; a treasury of pamphlets, prints, and ballads concerning a notorious Scottish body-snatching case in the early nineteenth century; and valuable first editions of Sigmund Freud's work on dreams.

The Academy of Medicine was founded in 1847 and moved to its present location in 1926. From its beginnings, the Academy has consistently been an effective advocate for public health and a major center for health education.

Above: The main reading room of the library of the Academy of Medicine. Opposite: Details from the exterior of the Academy of Medicine.

# BROOKLYN, QUEENS & STATEN ISLAND

# BROOKLYN FLEA

Schoolyard at Bishop Laughlin
Memorial High School
Lafayette Avenue
(between Vanderbilt and
Clermont Avenues)
Fort Greene, Brooklyn

Winter hibernation indoors
at DUMBO site; check website
www.brooklynflea.com

HOURS: Saturdays 10 am–5 pm

Going to a flea market on Saturday is as much a tradition in New York as it is in Paris. The newest and liveliest of the city's outdoor markets is the Brooklyn Flea, open every Saturday, rain or shine, from spring through autumn.

Like all such markets, the selection varies from week to week, with a potpourri of vintage clothing, garden tools, architectural salvage, eclectic furniture, silver spoons, sepia photos, and a mixture of bric-a-brac, odd collectibles, and an occasional treasure or two.

What makes the Brooklyn Flea even more interesting are the crafts sold here: handwoven textiles, hand-spun yarn, hand-thrown glazed-porcelain dinnerware, hand-embroidered pillows, hand-built wooden furniture, hand-sewn plaid pet coats, and a medley of hand-crafted silver bracelets. Forget any notions about handmade objects

being dull and earnest. These crafts have an inventiveness that makes even the handwrought radiator covers seem witty.

Best of all, the Brooklyn Flea is a gastronomic adventure. Try asparagus focaccia with parmesan or beans in a soy-wasabi brine. Stand in line for Salvadoran pupusas or Mexican huaraches. And if you have a sweet tooth, you've come to the right place: cannoli filled with fresh ricotta, sea-salted caramels, coconut cream pie, and red velvet cupcakes with lacy white frosting. After indulging in all that, you might want to stop by the booth that rents bicycles and take a spin around tree-lined Fort Greene.

Curios, cupcakes, and other small treasures at the Brooklyn Flea.

# NEW YORK
# TRANSIT MUSEUM

Corner of Boerum Place and
Schermerhorn Street
Downtown Brooklyn

718.694.1600
www.mta.info/mta/museum

HOURS: Tuesday–Friday 10 am–4 pm;
Saturday and Sunday 12 pm–5 pm

Subway buffs are crazy about the Transit Museum. So are urban historians and schoolchildren. More than six million riders travel on the New York City rapid transit system each weekday, although many of them have yet to discover this marvelous museum in Brooklyn. The city has 468 underground, elevated, and surface stations—plus the decommissioned subway station that now houses the Transit Museum. It is a perfect place to learn about the history of New York's public transportation. Its vast collection, impressive exhibitions, and intriguing programs help visitors explore the complex network of bridges, tunnels, commuter railroads, buses, and of course subways, the stars of the museum.

Twenty vintage subway and elevated cars—each like a time machine

Left: Detail of a mosaic tile in a subway station.
Opposite: Drawing by Tony Sarg from the 1920s,
depicting the 42nd Street subway station below
Grand Central Terminal.

that whisks you back to a long-ago
era—can be found on the museum's
lower level, ready to be boarded.
The earliest car dates from 1904, the
very year the subway was inaugurat-
ed. The original system was a monumental engineering feat that began
on Broadway at City Hall and head-
ed north to 145th Street, extending
the city en route. Today, 842 miles of
track stretch across New York City,
making this the largest subway system in the world and the only major
system open twenty-four hours a
day, every day of the year.

Straphangers are always fascinated by the story of the money
trains, those disguised work cars
staffed by armed agents who
collected revenue from the stations
each day. (Who can forget the movie
*The Taking of Pelham One Two Three?*)
The Transit Museum has organized

a popular exhibit that followed
the money collected from subway
turnstiles right to the bank. Times
change, and the MetroCard has now
eliminated any need for cash collectors or money trains.

The museum also has a small
annex at Grand Central Terminal
on 42nd Street, but serious subway
connoisseurs will head to Brooklyn
for full immersion in the gigantic
60,000-square-foot Transit Museum.
*Über*-enthusiasts will want to take
a museum-organized summer tour
to Coney Island, traveling on the
Nostalgia Train: a vintage car with
wicker upholstery, old-fashioned
lighting fixtures, and windows that
open to ocean breezes.

Above: Photo of the original IRT City Hall station,
1904. Opposite: Sixth Avenue with elevated tracks,
1901.

# P.S.1 CONTEMPORARY ART CENTER

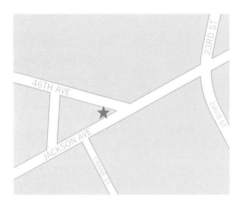

22-25 Jackson Avenue
(At the intersection of
Forty-Sixth Avenue)
Long Island City, Queens

718.784.2084
www.ps1.org

HOURS: Thursday–Monday 12 pm–6 pm

**A**nyone seriously interested in contemporary art tends to put P.S.1 at the top of the list of places to visit regularly. This is where to find the most innovative and adventurous art in the city—and it's evident the international art crowd has discovered it, too. There often seem to be as many visitors here from Berlin as from Brooklyn.

P.S.1 is affiliated with the Museum of Modern Art (MOMA), so the two institutions work closely to promote contemporary art through collaborative programs and exhibitions. Although P.S.1 is in Queens and MOMA is in Manhattan, the fact that they're only two subway stops apart (a short ride on the E or V trains) makes the distance seem much shorter. As the younger

Left: Detail of the 1890s museum building, originally a schoolhouse. Opposite: Panoramic view of P.S.1, its adjacent Queens neighborhood, and Manhattan's skyline across the river.

sibling in the relationship, P.S.1 is predictably brasher and more provocative in acting as a catalyst for new directions and ideas, whereas MoMA — as the world's leading modern art museum — gives a historical perspective through its vast collections. Rather than building a permanent collection, P.S.1 has chosen to concentrate on presenting an extensive number of temporary exhibitions each year.

It's unexpected to discover that P.S.1 and its cutting-edge art are located in an 1890s Romanesque-revival schoolhouse. The contrast between the art and the architecture works well, and all the building's unconventional spaces are utilized for exhibitions: classrooms, stairwells, long hallways, a janitor's closet, and even the boiler room in the basement. The constantly changing shows include site-specific installations, art from around the world, adventurous new work from recognized artists, and experimental work by emerging artists. As one blogger has written: "The exhibits are ephemeral, unlike the solid brick and stone building, but full of strange delights."

# THE NOGUCHI MUSEUM

32-37 Vernon Boulevard
Long Island City, Queens

718.204.7088
www.noguchi.org

HOURS: Wednesday–Friday 10 am–5 pm;
Saturday and Sunday 11 am–6 pm
(Be prepared: The museum is
a long walk from the subway)

The Noguchi Museum is a revelation to anyone visiting for the first time, or the fiftieth. Originally the studio of the distinguished sculptor Isamu Noguchi, the space is now a museum dedicated to his extraordinary art. Simple, lyrical, evocative, the museum itself is considered one of Noguchi's greatest works.

The building's minimalist spaces—its white brick walls and wood-beamed ceilings—are so spare that they seem to disappear, leaving only the eloquent sculpture. Beyond the galleries is the sculpture garden, the heart of the museum, inspired by the Japanese tradition in which a garden is considered on the same aesthetic level as painting or sculpture. Such a garden is "an art

Left: Detail of the garden at the Noguchi Museum.
Opposite: View of the museum interior.

object, valued for its own sake," noted an art critic, adding that it encourages a mood of meditative calm. Perhaps this explains why the garden at the Noguchi Museum invariably seems to be the most peaceful, serene place in New York City.

During his long life—from 1904 to 1988—Noguchi created sculptures from stone, ceramic, wood, bronze, and metal, as well as from the earth itself, in a scale ranging from the intimate to the monumental. He also designed paper lamps made of mulberry bark, children's playgrounds that inspire endless exploration, concrete bridges for Hiroshima, innovative furniture designs, vast landscape projects, experimental sculpture gardens, and theater sets for Martha Graham in which the sets became partners of the dancers. As Noguchi said, "Everything was sculpture. Any material, any idea."

Noguchi's dual heritage was reflected in his Eastern respect for nature and his Western interest in modernism. His father was a Japanese poet, his mother an American writer and schoolteacher. Although he spent his childhood in Japan, Noguchi returned to the United States as a teenager

and then had the good fortune to work in Constantin Brancusi's studio in Paris. As a young artist, he wrote that he wanted to be an interpreter of the East to the West through his sculpture. For much of his life he traveled between the two worlds and eventually commuted between dual studios: one on the island of Shikoku in Japan and the other in New York City, the studio that is now the Noguchi Museum. "Sculpture is infinitely complex," he said; "I am always learning, always discovering." And so can we all, in this extraordinary place.

Above: *Uruguayan*, granite sculpture in the garden of the Noguchi Museum. Opposite: Portrait of Isamu Noguchi next to his sculpture *Brilliance*, 1986.

# LITTLE INDIA IN JACKSON HEIGHTS

The #7 subway line stops at so many ethnic neighborhoods in Queens that it's known as the "international express." Passengers getting off a train at the Roosevelt Avenue station in Jackson Heights are often en route to Little India, a lively commercial center for the city's Southeast Asian community.

Walking along a block-long stretch of 74th Street—from Roosevelt to 37th Avenue—takes you past shop after shop selling exotic wares. Himalayan dumplings, Hindu dictionaries, cricket bats, DVDs of the latest Bollywood films. Exquisite saris and bolts of fabric in a rainbow of colors. Cardamom, coriander, and a profusion of spices. Carved statues of Ganesh, the elephant god. A dazzling array of gold jewelry: intricately designed 22-karat necklaces, rings, and bracelets, often delicately filigreed. Sitars, tabla drums, and other musical instruments. An amazing food market—Patel Brothers—with shelves bursting with fifty-pound bags of Basmati rice, chickpeas and lentils, jars of ghee, lotus root, mango pulp, and a multiplicity of chutneys. Spending an hour or two on 74th Street can seem like a sojourn in Bombay.

Nearly half of the population in Queens is foreign born, so it's not surprising that 138 languages are spoken here. The diversity is astonishing in every neighborhood. Just a short walk from 74th Street—or an even shorter ride on the #7 subway—live families from Colombia, Ecuador, Peru, Argentina, and Mexico, as well as China and Korea. All are as eager to share their cultures and cuisines as those who welcome visitors to Little India's exuberant enclave.

74th Street, between Roosevelt
and 37th Avenues
Jackson Heights, Queens

Above and left: Shopping on 74th Street in
Jackson Heights.

# LOUIS ARMSTRONG HOUSE MUSEUM

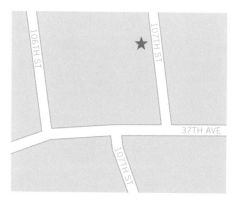

34–56 107th Street
Corona, Queens

Subway: #7 to 103rd Street;
directions on Website
718.478.8274
www.louisarmstronghouse.org

HOURS: Tuesday–Friday 10 am–5 pm;
Saturday and Sunday 12 pm–5 pm

---

Opposite: Louis Armstrong in an impromptu
concert on his front steps, surrounded by
young neighbors.

Next page, above: Portrait of Louis Armstrong,
1931. Below left: LeBlanc trumpet with
"Satchmo Louis Armstrong" written in
raised letters on bell. Below right: Louis and
Lucille's home in Corona, now the Louis
Armstrong House Museum.

Louis Armstrong is celebrated as the greatest jazz musician of all time. His dazzling virtuosity on the trumpet and innovative style of singing set a new standard for music. Satchmo—a nickname from his early days as a trumpeter—was acclaimed internationally, yet his home in Queens is as unpretentious as the man himself.

This small house, now a national historic landmark, has been restored to the way it was when Armstrong and his wife, Lucille, lived there. In 1943, he was off on a tour performing—as he did for more than three hundred days each year—when Lucille surprised him by buying this house. He loved being part of the Corona neighborhood and having his hair cut at Joe's Artistic Barber Shop two blocks away, or being encircled by children when giving

an impromptu concert on his front steps. Today, the Louis Armstrong House Museum and Archives are part of Queens College.

Jazz fans and anyone who has ever listened to any of Satchmo's recordings will love taking a tour of the house. Lucille had every room redesigned, creating a dramatic seventy-foot-long living room for entertaining, a kitchen with stylish turquoise lacquered cabinets, and a bathroom covered from floor to ceiling in mirrors (so fabulous that it was featured in *Time* magazine). But the den belonged entirely to Louis Armstrong; this is where he wrote his autobiography, recorded audiotapes, typed letters to his fans, designed inventive collages, and visited with musicians.

Armstrong was fascinated by technology and always owned the best audio equipment available. While performing around the world, he traveled with a trunk holding reel-to-reel tape decks and a turntable for listening to music that ranged from Jelly Roll Morton to Tchaikovsky. At home, he used hundreds of seven-inch reels to record conversations, interviews, reminiscences, and sometimes the sound of a trumpet. Hearing these tapes as you tour the house is an incredible surprise. Imagine:

You're in the Armstrongs' dining room listening to a dialogue taped during a long-ago dinner with Louis and Lucille and their friends, hearing the sound of laughter, the clink of silverware, a dog barking, a joke or two, and the inimitable raspy voice of Satchmo.

In 1971, Louis Armstrong died at home in Queens, mourned by millions. He was born in New Orleans in 1901 into harsh poverty, in a neighborhood so dangerous it was called "The Battleground." His musical genius would take him on a long and extraordinary journey, from a stretch in the Colored Waif's Home for Boys and performing in a small riverboat orchestra, to Carnegie Hall and performances all over the world. The French named a street after him in Paris (*Place Louis Armstrong*, in the 13th arrondissement). The U.S. State Department sent him abroad as an ambassador, bringing jazz to audiences from Africa to South America. His influence as a musician, singer, composer, and cultural icon remains unmatched. Perhaps his friend Duke Ellington described him best when he said that Satchmo was "beyond category."

# JAMAICA BAY WILDLIFE REFUGE

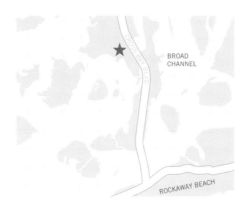

BROAD CHANNEL

ROCKAWAY BEACH

Cross Bay Boulevard
Broad Channel, Queens

718.318.4340
www.nps.gov/gate
Directions: Take the A train
to Queens; one stop after
JFK Airport

HOURS: Daily 8:30 am–5 pm
Closed Thanksgiving Day, Christmas Day,
New Year's Day

The Jamaica Bay Wildlife Refuge is a spectacular place for bird watching, with more than 9,000 acres of salt marshes and ponds, fields and woods, an open expanse of bay, and five miles of trails. Thousands of birds stop over during their spring and autumn migrations; many stay to build nests and raise their young in the protected reeds and grasses. More than 330 avian species have been recorded here, traveling from as far south as South America and as far north as the Arctic.

The bird log at the Visitors Center records hand-written lists of sightings that are jotted down day by day throughout the year. A great number of birds are listed during the first week of May: scarlet tanager,

Left: One of the thousands of birds that visit this Wildlife Sanctuary each year. Opposite: Detail of nautical chart of Jamaica Bay.

Above: House on stilts in Broad Channel.
Below left: More than 330 species of birds have
been recorded in this Wildlife Sanctuary.
Below right: A comfortable birdhouse. Opposite:
Spectacular bird watching in New York City.

black-billed cuckoo, glossy ibis, orchard oriole, tricolored heron, red-breasted grosbeak, rufous towhee, tree swallows, oystercatcher, white-crowned sparrow, spotted sandpiper, goldfinch, bobolink, a bald eagle, and many more, including a dozen types of warblers.

The National Park Service does a heroic job managing and protecting the Jamaica Bay estuary to ensure the survival of migrating birds. Even endangered species such as the pere-grine falcon live here, and the glossy ibis returned after disappearing from New York for more than ninety years. After being declared extinct, the snowy egret also came back; a colony of these birds now lives at the refuge.

Part of the fascination of visiting the Jamaica Bay Wildlife Refuge is that it can be reached by subway. Take the A train to Broad Channel, a small town that began as a fishing village in the 1880s and became a notorious rum-running nightspot during Prohibition in the 1920s. Today, it's a quiet community that seems far away from the rest of the city, with boats parked in driveways and houses perched on stilts over the water.

How amazing that one of the best bird-watching locations in the Western Hemisphere is located half a mile from the subway. Even more surreal, Kennedy Airport is visible from the refuge. Airplanes and shorebirds can be seen nimbly gliding to landings, composing a unique aerial ballet over Jamaica Bay.

# ALICE AUSTEN
# HOUSE MUSEUM

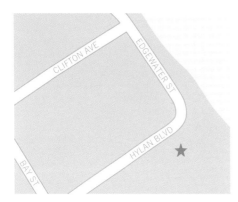

2 Hylan Boulevard
Staten Island

Directions: Staten Island Ferry,
then take S51 bus or taxi
718.816.4506
www.aliceausten.org

HOURS: Thursday–Sunday 12 pm–5 pm
Closed January, February, and
major holidays

This enchanting, small Victorian cottage, perched at the water's edge overlooking New York's harbor, is so delightful that it feels like a new discovery every time you visit. This was the home of the remarkable photographer Alice Austen, who lived here almost her entire life. Now a museum, the house— and Austen's photographs—evoke a world long since vanished.

Alice Austen was one of the earliest women photographers in America. She was born in 1866, became fascinated by photography as a young girl, and for the next half-century took thousands of

Left: The Victorian cottage where Alice Austen lived for most of her life. Opposite: Alice Austen's 1890 photograph of children on the beach in front of her home (note the four-masted schooner sailing by).

images. More than 3,000 of her glass-plate negatives have survived; many of the photographs show her family and friends enjoying carefree musical evenings, masquerades, and bicycling along the shore roads of Staten Island, then an enclave for the wealthy. Details are sharply recorded, whether the sails of a schooner or a tennis racquet held askew.

Her longtime companion, Gertrude Tate—they were together for more than fifty years—attributed Austen's success in photography to a combination of artistry and sheer stubbornness of will. She became best known for her "street photography," creating vivid portraits of rag pickers, young shoeshine boys, pushcart vendors, fishmongers at Fulton Market, children selling newspapers, and immigrants newly arrived at Battery Park with their baggage in hand. Her photographs portray the less fortunate with a striking sense of dignity.

Sadly, Austen was overwhelmed by adversity during the last years of her life. With the crash of the stock market in 1929, this independent, spirited woman lost all that remained of her inheritance. Desperate, she sold valuable possessions, opened a tea room on the front lawn, and finally mortgaged her beloved home. The story grew sadder as she was evicted and forced to live in the poorhouse. And then, miraculously, her glass-plate negatives were discovered and some of the photographs were published. Her last year was spent in comfort before her death in 1952.

Today, Austen's ancestral home has been restored. Her grandfather had purchased the property in 1844, transforming a tumbledown farmhouse into a romantic country villa. Picturesque dormers were added, crowned with birdhouse finials, and the eaves were extended to create a shady vine-covered porch. The house, named Clear Comfort by her grandmother, once again looks like the home Alice Austen lived in for eighty years. It's no wonder she loved the garden and its lavender wisteria, the upstairs darkroom where she printed her photographs, and the view from the front windows of ships sailing by.

# CHINESE SCHOLAR'S GARDEN

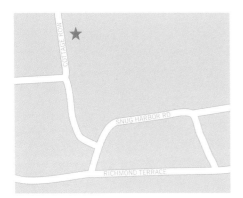

Snug Harbor
1000 Richmond Terrace
Staten Island

Directions: Staten Island Ferry,
then take S40 bus or taxi to
Snug Harbor
718.273.8200
www.sibg.org/cg

HOURS: (April 1–October 31) Tuesday–
Sunday 10 am–5 pm; (November 1–March 31)
Tuesday–Sunday 12 pm–4 pm

**B**reathtaking in its beauty, the New York Chinese Scholar's Garden was inspired by classic Chinese gardens of the past, particularly those of the fabled Ming dynasty (1368–1644). Its complex design dramatically creates the illusion of infinite space through an unfolding series of courtyards, ponds, and pavilions — a composition found in Chinese scroll painting as well as in this exquisite garden.

The design is based on the principles of yin–yang, in which harmony is achieved through a unity of opposing concepts. The contrasts are everywhere: the interplay of light and shadow in the views from a moon gate; the varied shapes of creviced rocks in a courtyard and

Left: View through an intricate patterned window at the Chinese Scholar's Garden. Opposite: A pavilion for contemplation or viewing the moon.

Above and opposite: Exquisite views of pavilions, ponds, and hidden vistas in the Chinese Scholar's Garden.

the smooth round pebbles underfoot; the splashing waterfalls and the still water of the ponds; the serenity within the garden and the clamor of the world outside.

Take time to understand the intricacy of the design. Walk across a bridge built just inches high to experience the illusion of walking on water. Decipher the meaning of the plants and trees; discover that the pine, plum, and bamboo symbolize "three friends in the winter season, aloof, proud, and enduring." Learn how to interpret hidden views, unfolding behind a screen or wall, and borrowed views, which include distant vistas and even the sky above.

This spectacular garden on Staten Island was created in the late 1990s by a group of forty Chinese artists and artisans from Suzhou, a city famous for its gardens. They relied on traditional time-honored methods for construction (not a single nail was used). Sculptured rocks were transported from a river near Suzhou, and many of the architectural elements—such as the bridges and the pavilions' roof tiles—were crafted in China.

It's said that a fifteenth-century garden builder, Ji Ching, advised that a garden is "created by the human hand, but should appear as if created by heaven."

# INDEX OF PLACES

Above: "The Proposed Chrystie-Forsyth Parkway,"
1930. The Regional Plan Association. The
Skyscraper Museum.

# ILLUSTRATION CREDITS

**All photographs are by Alexandra Stonehill except for the following:** 2: drawing courtesy of the High Line; 17: panoramic collage courtesy of Poets House; 18-21: photos by Robert Polidori, and vintage drawing and photos, courtesy of the Skyscraper Museum; 26: photo courtesy of the Museum of American Finance; 40-43: MOCA images from their archives and rendering from the Maya Lin Studio; 44-46: photos by Kate Milford, courtesy of Museum at Eldridge Street; 56: photo by Jook-Leung, courtesy of Merchant's House Museum; 63: vintage photo from the Byron Collection at MCNY; 68: photo courtesy of Film Forum; 69-71: photos and drawing courtesy of Center for Architecture; 76-79: drawings and archival photos courtesy of the High Line; 82-85: photos courtesy of Rubin Museum of Art; 86-89: photos courtesy of the Museum at FIT; 96: map drawn and engraved by M. Rapkin, c. 1850, from the NYPL Map Collection; 98-99: photos courtesy of Campbell Apartment; 103-6: photos courtesy of the Japan Society; 110-13: photos courtesy of the Grolier Club; 117-119: photos courtesy of the Nicholas Roerich Museum; 125-26: photos courtesy of The Hispanic Society of America; 132-135: photo by Susan DeVries and vintage print courtesy of the Dyckman Farmhouse; 140: WPA poster from the Library of Congress; 142: book jacket from the NYPL collection; 144: photo from the Byron Collection at MCNY; 145: photo by Samuel H. Gottscho Collection at MCNY; 146-47: photos

from the Berenice Abbott Collection at MCNY (preceding four images courtesy of MCNY); 151: photo courtesy of the New York Academy of Medicine; 157: drawing by Tony Sarg, 1920s; 161: photo by Elizabeth Felicella, courtesy of P.S.1; 162: photo of Damian Ortega's sculpture *Controller of the Universe*, courtesy of Collection Glenn Fuhrman, the FLAG Art Foundation, and P.S.1; 164: photo by Shigeo Angai courtesy of the Noguchi Museum; 165: photo by Elizabeth Felicella, courtesy of the Noguchi Museum; 166: photo of Isamu Noguchi by Shigeo Anzai, 1986, courtesy of the Noguchi Museum; 167: photo of *Uruguayan*, sculpture by Isamu Noguchi, photo by Michio Noguchi, courtesy of the Noguchi Museum; 171-72: archival photos courtesy of the Louis Armstrong House Museum; 179-180: vintage photo photos courtesy of the Alice Austen House Museum; 187: drawing courtesy of the Skyscraper Museum. Any other maps, vintage photos, and drawings are from private collections.

---

Right: Spring blossoms in the Garden at St. Luke's in the Fields.

Next page: A serene corner at The Cloisters.

Page 2: The High Line.

Page 4: Brooklyn Flea.

# ACKNOWLEDGMENTS

First published in the United States of
America in 2009 by Universe Publishing
A Division of Rizzoli
International Publications, Inc.
300 Park Avenue South, New York, NY 10010
www.rizzoliusa.com

Designed by Willy Wong

Rizzoli Editor: Ellen R. Cohen

ISBN: 978-0-7893-2011-7
Library of Congress Control Number:
2009925261

Printed in China

2009 2010 2011 2012 2013 / 10 9 8 7 6 5 4 3 2 1

New York's Unique and Unexpected Places is
part of a series of New York Bound books.

Many thanks to those who generously participated
in this project: Kristin Aguilera, Baltsar Beckeld,
Rick Bell, Michael Cogswell, Heidi B. Coleman,
Karen Cooper, Sean Corcoran, Susan DeVries,
Daniel Entin, Stephen Facey, Cheri Fein,
Margaret Halsey Gardiner, Melina Gills, Wendy
Gleason, Josh Hamilton, Eric Holzenberg, Alice
C. Hudson, April Hunt, Susan Henshaw Jones,
Shannon Jowett, Sandra Kingsbury, Cynthia
Kracauer, Sam Quan Krueger, Amy Stein Milford,
Peter Mullan, Jane Preston, G. Carl Rutberg,
Alanna Schindewolf, Daniel Silva, Carol Willis,
Suzanne Wise, Lesley Zlabinger.

To everyone on the Rizzoli team, thanks and
appreciation — particularly to Willy Wong, so
talented a designer, and Ellen Rosefsky Cohen,
an extraordinary editor.

Special thanks to this book's first readers, all
quintessential New Yorkers and dear friends:
Barbara Cohen, Ellen Sargent, and Mia Ting.
Very special thanks to David Stonehill, who read
each page more times than he'd care to count.

To Ethan Hawke, with thanks for the great
foreword — so edgy and lyrical, just like New York.

# NOTES